BEYOND YOGA TEACHER TRAINING:

HOW TO TEACH WITH CONFIDENCE

JEN VALLENS

CONTENTS

INTRODUCTION

Congratulations on your completion of yoga teacher training! You may be thinking, now what? It's normal to question where to go next in your teaching journey. Even though you are a certified yoga teacher, it's common to feel as if you are ill prepared to teach yoga **FOR REAL**.

I wrote this book to help guide you through the process of putting your training into practice. And second, to instill in you a belief that you have what it takes to be anything you want...even a yoga teacher!

Think of it as a supplement or a reference manual, something you can come back to time and time again. Think of me as your mentor, a cheerleader, a guide, and a friend who is here to support you on your teaching journey.

Although yoga teacher training is a wonderful experience, it cannot fully replicate what occurs inside the yoga studio class. When teaching yoga, there are many balls to juggle. You have to consider your sequence, your music, the lighting, the volume of of the music, how the students are reacting, and of course, your beginner nerves.

If you feel as if you are not prepared or confident enough to take your training to the next level and start teaching, please know that I felt the exact same way when I completed teacher training. This wasn't because my training was insufficient. It was because of where I was in my personal life. They say that yoga teacher training is a journey and that is true. It's a journey to learn this marvelous ancient practice, but also a journey of self-exploration.

It was not until I hit my 40s when I decided I needed a change in my life. I took stock of what was and was not working for me. I was tired of dieting, people pleasing, feeling guilty, allowing fear to stop me from doing certain things, and an overall feeling of anxiousness.

In keeping with my new yoga training, I developed a mantra: "Why NOT Me?" I repeated it to myself daily. Every time I was faced with feelings of insecurity or doubt, I would repeat *Why NOT Me?* and my thinking shifted. I looked for challenges to overcome rather than avoid. I started with a fitness challenge at my gym and lost 8% body fat and learned healthier ways to eat and exercise.

I developed other mantras to help me in my journey of self-improvement and as a yoga teacher. These include:

- *Plant Seeds and Lead by Example*
- *You Can't Until You Can*
- *Sometimes, but not Always*

I realized that I was interested in yoga and had participated in classes, but it wasn't a *way of life* — a *practice*. Like many, I felt indulgent when I went to a yoga class as if I didn't deserve to take time for myself. I thought doing yoga took time away from my kids and other responsibilities. I also didn't see yoga in the same light as my fitness routine, so I chose fitness. Now, I know that yoga is not an indulgence, but rather, a necessary means of self care. Yoga is not only a physical practice in self care, but a mental one. I found that practicing yoga was a lot less expensive and far more effective than the $150 per hour I paid to a therapist.

When I started taking classes, I was not looking to teach yoga. But I happened upon a class at CorePower Yoga in which the teacher spoke about Yoga Sculpt teacher training and I heard my mantra sound in my head... *Why NOT Me?* With a mere 10 yoga classes under my belt, I launched into Yoga Sculpt teaching training.

I completed the training and enjoyed it so much, I then signed up for Power Training and after that, Hot Power Fusion training. In spite of all this training, I still had no plans to teach, but I felt I needed to challenge myself and audition for a teaching job with CorePower Yoga.

Drumroll please... I didn't get the job. Even though I never envisioned myself teaching, I still felt defeated. The rejection stung, particularly after holding my mantra close to my heart. However, I continued with my practice and to my surprise, two years later, I received a call to see if I would be interested in auditioning again to teach Yoga Sculpt. After that second audition, I received an offer and I have been teaching at CorePower Yoga ever since.

But I have to share that teaching yoga did not come easy for me. Overcoming my fear of public speaking and trusting myself as a teacher remains a continual process. The reason I teach and continue to "put myself out there" is because it helps me to grow as a person and provides me with a forum to inspire others, and that is important to me.

My intention with teaching is to provide an environment where students feel a sense of belonging. If I can use my platform to help even one person feel safe and supported to explore their own mind and body, then I know I have done my job.

Yoga has helped me to understand myself better. Finding acceptance for myself while still striving for improvement is a challenge. But it is an important part of growth and a message that I impart on my students. More importantly, it is something that I personally practice and strive for every day.

Now, ten years later, I find myself in another *Why NOT Me* moment. Writing a book has been on my bucket list for as long as I can remember. Although I have had many first starts, it is only now with life experience and gained perspective, that I decided to take the leap. I've become comfortable with mistakes I've made and have learned from them. Through my trials, I have grown. It is through my practice that I have become wiser.

It is not always easy for me to embrace my *Flawsomeness*. It is a daily practice. I repeat: It is a daily PRACTICE. Some days are easier than others. But yoga helps me live my life. My hope with this book is that sharing my passion for teaching yoga will help other teachers find their passion, lose doubt, and build self-confidence.

My role as a yoga instructor is to inspire others and guide them safely through their practice. My role is not to teach per se, but rather to guide students to explore their own minds and bodies, and follow their own intuition. I can only 'Plant Seeds and Lead by Example'. I return to this mantra when I lead a class as well as in my personal life when I find myself frustrated by unmet expectations from myself or others.

The truth is most of us are doing the best we can at any given time. The key is to realize that each day is different and it is essential to stop ourselves from jumping on our soapbox when we are up and not berate ourselves when we are down.

Another mantra that keeps me on track is simply stating, "Sometimes, but not Always." These simple, four words can bring me back from the depths of self-annihilation. My daily yoga practice is imperative for my mental health. In other words, it's my method for challenging my inner bully when she calls me names as well as keeping my ego in check.

But let me explain why I choose the seat of teacher. I am not a Master Yogi. I have had a personal practice for seven years, and yet, I still cannot "fly my crow". I do not have a graceful dancer's body and cannot send my leg over my head in a perfect standing bow. But in all honesty, this doesn't matter to me. To me, yoga is not about getting somewhere or mastering something. It is about living my best life. I teach yoga to inspire others to be their own teachers. I wrote this book to offer support and encouragement, and to help motivate you to look within yourself and find out why YOU want to teach.

To be clear, this book is far from a "how to" book. If you expect a blueprint or recipe on ways to be happy, more successful, find inner peace, or get better at flying your crow, this is not the intention behind this book. I am not an expert, guru, or master. But I've had a journey through teacher training and beyond that matches the experience of many other yogis. I'm here to share my story and help you lead your optimum life as a yoga teacher. My aim is to plant seeds and lead by example, both as a yoga teacher and a human.

You will recall we end our yoga classes with "Namaste — the divine (or fill in the blank) in me honors and sees the divine (fill in the blank) in you. When we are both in this place of authenticity, we truly exist as one." My favorite fill in the blank phrase is, The FLAWSOME in me honors and sees the FLAWSOME in you."

When I completed my training and did not get the job, I felt deflated. In fact, I felt like a complete failure. At the same time, I did not feel ready to teach following training. I felt like a fraud and I lacked self-confidence. But I would not let that stop me. I continued with my personal, daily practice and embarked on more self-study. I journaled, bought books and watched videos. I started teaching yoga to kids as an after-school enrichment program.

There were so many times that I felt I wasn't good enough or that I had wasted my time and money on yoga teacher training. During training and auditions I let myself believe that someone else's opinion of me gave me an identity. I spent endless nights worried about receiving approval from others and doubting myself.

But thankfully, I refused to be so discouraged by not getting the job that I burned bridges or decided to stop practicing altogether. Instead, I kept up my practice. It paid off because now I teach for that same studio and I'm here to share my experience with you.

This book is designed to be a springboard for self-reflection and help you discover who you are as a teacher. I encourage you to find out what only you can bring to your students in an authentic manner.

I cannot promise that after reading my book you will take center stage like a rock star. However, the advice and real world scenarios I discuss are designed to lessen your nerves and help you form your identity, not only on your mat, but in your life as well.

I now see nerves simply as a sign that one cares. I questioned if I belonged in teacher training, let alone in front of a class. But, if I can do it, so can you. Think of me as your mentor, cheerleader, and friend who supports you on your yoga journey.

CHAPTER ONE

PREPARING TO TEACH

THINGS AREN'T ALWAYS what they seem.

This adage can be said about numerous pursuits including teaching yoga. Don't get me wrong; I love what I do and look forward to all of my classes. But did I expect to spend hours outside of work making playlists and learning sequences? Did I think teaching yoga would be hard? No, to all of the above. And yet, I still love my job.

Teaching yoga is hard work, which is why I've written this book to help pave that initial bumpy road for new teachers. My goal is to illustrate some real life scenarios that you should be aware of, but perhaps hadn't considered. These fall into a number of topics ranging from safety to marketing – things that new teachers, who are typically only focused on sequencing, sometimes forget.

UNIQUELY YOU

It's not easy to put into practice your yoga teacher training. It's even harder to do so and be unique. Throughout the book, I'll remind you to find your niche as a teacher, and what makes you You!

Each chapter of this book builds upon the previous one to help you develop your focus and refine your teaching goals. I'll discuss how to identify what makes you unique beyond other teachers, how to structure your class, and how to find students who resonate with your teaching style.

To guide you each step of the way and ensure your success, I've included self-reflective exercises, sequencing templates, and other tools to put your teacher training into practice.

FIRST THINGS FIRST

To help you launch into this book and your goal of becoming a more confident teacher, I suggest you create a binder. Disorganization is the death of any project. I don't know about you, but I get a great deal of satisfaction from sorting and putting things in their place.

However, this does not come naturally for me. I am what you call one of those "creative types". You might cringe if you saw the state of my wallet or my nightstand drawer at any given moment. To be effective and avoid missing important deadlines, I have learned that I must organize my projects.

I have come to accept that my life is exceptionally messy. Having been diagnosed with ADD as an adult, it now makes perfect sense why I have both a lack of order and a desperate need for order. If I do not sort and categorize, I will inevitably be late and lost. So, I have created a binder for every job I have ever had. This has been one of the greatest tools that I now share with you.

I suggest using a 3-ring binder with some dividers. Title your dividers as anything that make sense to you. The following sections are examples of what you might include.

ABOUT ME -

This is the section for your bio. Don't worry; I will give you an exercise on how to write it. You will develop it by asking yourself some serious questions that will help you hone in on your niche. As you teach and complete this bio exercise, you may be surprised to discover your niche is different than you originally thought.

SEQUENCES -

I start with a blank template and make a bunch of copies. You can choose to use mine or come up with one of your own. I like to keep a print-out of all of my sequences to keep track. You may forgo the binder and prefer to keep a journal instead. Finding what works for you is the key.

You will determine what makes sense for you. But whatever you choose, it's a good idea to initially keep your sequences in order so that you may return to them along with making notes as to what worked and what didn't. I like to also include feedback from students I have received.

INSPIRATION -

This is where I keep quotes, theme ideas, and songs for future classes.

REFERENCE -

If you find an article or something that you want to incorporate into your class or research further, it is good to have a running list.

CONTACTS -

Chances are you will keep your contacts electronically, but I think it is helpful to have a printout. You may want to include a list of local studios and manager contacts as well as names and contact information for each student who attends your class.

. . .

*C*ALENDAR -

This is a good place to keep track of your hours and schedule if you are working in multiple environments and have private clients.

*A*CCOUNTING -

Keep a running log of your earnings (both for the studio you work for and private clients) and outgoings (yoga clothes, continuing education, CPR certification, etc).

NOW THAT YOU HAVE YOUR BINDER SET UP, LET'S TALK about YOU.

CHAPTER TWO

HOW TO BE UNIQUELY YOU

IT'S ALL PEACHY... I'm a big fan of analogies and use them in my class quite a bit. Cheesy? Perhaps... but also effective. So here goes... I love peaches. Yet, it doesn't matter that I find them to be juicy, perfect, and delicious. There will always be someone who simply doesn't like the taste of peaches. You cannot blame a person for not liking peaches. You cannot force or talk a person into liking peaches. Someone who does not like peaches, may never like the taste of peaches. However, they may be really into strawberries or mango or pineapple. The way I see it, a peach is not a superior fruit. It is no better or more worthy a fruit than a strawberry or a pineapple. It is simply different. Just the same, the person eating the fruit is not right or wrong for preferring peaches.

You can see where I'm going with this analogy. If you compare yourself to others and get insecure as a result, you must stop. There is no comparing in yoga, not among students or teachers. Each person is different. Stop trying to be a peach and instead focus on being the freshest, tastiest version of YOU.

I held this analogy close to my heart while reading Sarah Knight's book, *You Do You: How to be Who You Are and Use What You've Got to Get What You Want.* I recommend it, but if you don't have time to read it, there is one important message that she imparts and I will share:

There is nothing wrong with you.

Embrace Feedback

After I had been teaching at CorePower Yoga for awhile, a co-worker took my Yoga Sculpt class. I remember feeling nervous at the prospect of another teacher taking my class out of fear of being judged and compared. Now, I welcome that opportunity.

But in my early teaching days, I was easily intimidated. My biggest Yoga Sculpt teaching challenge was staying on beat and this had been a criticism — a "need for improvement" or the "grow" in the sandwich feedback formula used by managers at the studio.

I awaited comments from the teacher after class and surprisingly, found her words to be supportive and comforting. My co-worker, Riley, said she loved my class and my energy. She liked that it was different and her advice or rather, her parting words that evening were: "Whatever you do, keep doing YOU."

I had heard the same sentiment in self-help books. Do You....and it always sounded so cheesy. But when my peer, Riley, spoke those words to me, the message resonated. I needed to stop trying to teach like other teachers and instead, teach in a style that was authentic to me. Most importantly, I had to be okay with being who I am.

The students who "get" me and like my style will come back; those who don't, won't. Not everyone is going to like you. And that is okay.

However, there is a difference between knowing this intellectually and allowing it to penetrate your belief system. Too often, we resort back to feeling less than and trying to "fix" what we perceive to be wrong.

Sometimes forming acceptance of who we are seems to be at odds with working toward a better version of ourselves. Your yoga practice can help bridge these two ideas to help you simultaneously accept where you are and work toward a higher goal.

UNDERSTAND YOUR 'WHY'

How do you know where you want to go in yoga and life? First, you need to become aware of where you are and how you got here. You need to be completely clear on your WHY. Why are you headed in the direction you are going? Why do you want to get there? Why do you hope to find something that isn't available now? Yes, these are deep questions. Yet, without self-awareness, there is no growth.

We all have an inner guide or internal compass that points us toward our core values. The problem is that for most of our life, we were taught to ignore many natural instincts such as 'don't cry' and 'don't touch'. We were told to smile and be quiet. We stopped learning to trust our gut feelings. These messages became ingrained in our neural pathways and instead of trusting the warning signs that something was not congruent with our core values, we bypass anxious feelings, ignore them, or numb them. However, that anxious feeling always comes back.

Yoga is a way to practice getting in touch with our inner emotions and trust ourselves. When we can bring our core values into our consciousness, we can begin to live purposefully.

FIND YOUR CORE VALUE

Core values are the guiding principles that dictate your thoughts and behavior. When you are clear on what it is you value, every decision you are confronted with will become easier. And, if you still struggle with a decision, perhaps it means there isn't a wrong choice, just a hard one. You might simply need to make the decision... whichever it is and move on.

When we are clear on our core values, it serves as a guide to help us persevere. Even if our pursuit is scary, boring, frustrating, (fill in the blank), we do what we do because we know who we are and what will bring us closer to the best version of ourselves.

This chapter will illustrate how believing in yourself helps to build your self-esteem. To quote Henry Ford, "Whether you think you can or think you can't, you are right!"

I know you want to be more confident when you teach yoga or you would not have picked up this book. But let me be clear, reading this book will not make you a better yoga teacher. But reading this book and doing the exercises may help you determine why you want to teach yoga and how you can be the best version of yourself.

This book will help you uncover your core values and bring your unique talents to the surface so that you can live a more inspired life. That may include teaching yoga or it may not. But I know this....if you want to teach yoga, you can.

This book is about helping you gain confidence. I guarantee that will happen in time. You need to believe in yourself.

DON'T STAND IN YOUR OWN WAY

I used to be one of those people who would pray at night (even though I am not religious) and it would go something like this: "Oh please God, just let me get the job," "Lose 10 pounds," (fill in the blank,) and I will be happy and never ask for another thing.

I used to check my horoscope daily to see if I was going to have a good day. I attended workshops and read books from Anthony Robbins and followed diet programs filled with promises. But it wasn't until I practiced yoga consistently that I realized the only person who could make myself feel different, to accomplish the things I dreamt about, and do the things that I admired in others...was ME. Coincidently, the only person standing in my way was also ME.

Yoga for me is about so much more than moving my body and

quieting my mind; it also feeds my soul. It is a way of life and if you completed yoga teaching training and have been practicing for any length of time, you probably have seen ways your life has changed since introducing yoga into it as well. Maybe you are a little more tolerant of others. Maybe you stop yourself in the heat of the moment to pause and breathe. Maybe you challenge any "I'm not good enough" thoughts. If you've made these positive changes due to yoga, then you should also believe that yoga will help you overcome your fear of teaching.

Being a successful yoga teacher simply requires you to find your inner guide and do some serious self study, in Sanskrit known as Svadhyaya, one of the Niyamas in Patanjali's Yoga Sutras, and of course practice.

I AM NOT AN EXPERT AT LIFE. NEWSFLASH... NOBODY IS! But I am an expert at my own life and I have set the stage for my life story, one that I want to see play out. I have intentionally cast myself in the starring role. I am becoming my own hero and I hope to inspire you to do the same.

You might ask how do you discover your core values? It starts first by finding your mantra. Your personal mantra is one of the keys to finding your purpose and living an inspired life.

As I discussed earlier, my yoga teaching journey began with a simple mantra... Why NOT Me? Let's find yours.

A mantra is a word, phrase, or chant that is repeated either out loud or in your mind.

The benefits of a mantra are manifold. A mantra serves as a motivating anchor to keep you focused and the repetition puts your mind in a meditative state, calming your nervous system while sealing the message into your subconscious.

Even mundane everyday activities can result in this calming state when performed repetitively. Maybe you experience this calm while doing dishes, folding laundry, or repeating patterns when knitting or something similar.

Try this tactic to access a calm nature through repetition. Visualize the continuous rise and fall of ocean waves along with the repetitive sound of the waves crashing. Repetition lets your mind rest by quieting the inner chatter. Your mind begins to enter a meditative state.

FINDING YOUR MANTRA

To find your mantra, we need to become aware of what we want to experience more of. Is it joy? Is it achievement? Is it connection? Is it knowledge?

A good way to determine what we need is to listen to our inner dialog. What is that nagging voice inside your head saying to you? Is it calling you names? This inner critic or inner bully will be your best guide of what it is that you want to change. Our brains are wired to look for repetition and patterns for optimum efficiency.

The more something is repeated, such as an activity or thought, the more it will be on autopilot. This allows our brains to focus on creating new neural pathways. That is why when we continue to put ourselves in new situations where learning can occur, our brain must figure out how to sort that new information.

Our brain will try to default to our old way of doing and seeing things. This is because it's comfortable; it is known and familiar. The same is true of the messages we tell ourselves.

CHALLENGE YOUR INNER BULLY

Our ego will do everything it can to make sure our behavior matches our thoughts and convinces us that we are right. This is a self-fulfilling prophecy. The only way to break this cycle is to challenge your inner bully.

If your inner bully says, "You are not good enough," challenge that statement with the counter sentiment: "I am enough!" I am happy to share that mantra with you until you adopt one of your own.

Furthermore, the concept of positive thinking or creating a personal mantra, isn't simply a feel-good exercise. There exists scientific evidence to back up the idea that when we circumvent a negative thought and replace it with a positive one, and do so repeatedly, we can actually change our brains. This is called Neuroplasticity.

The process allows us to "un-do" negative thoughts while embedding a new, more positive mindset into our subconscious. When I aim to accomplish this phenomenon, I rely on my personal, favorite mantras that I shared with you earlier.

Again, these are:

- Why NOT Me
- Plant Seeds and Lead by Example
- You Can't until you Can
- Sometimes, but Not Always

If ever a nagging voice tries to mess with you and starts egging you on, borrow one of my mantras. Within those phrases, you have a retort. I AM ENOUGH... I AM ENOUGH... I AM ENOUGH!

LOSE YOUR IDENTITY TO FIND IT

Life is uncertain and can be messy. Because of this, we as humans try to make sense of it. We try to place things, ideas, people, etc. into boxes to categorize and sort them. We try to find a place where everything fits and belongs. We give ourselves "identities" and "labels" so that we feel more in control of what is uncertain. We look for familiar patterns so that we can predict behavior and make sense of events.

I have shifted my mindset from "I am a yoga teacher" to "I teach yoga." This may seem like a minor change in semantics, but it is the difference between being attached to an identity or being free and open to all possibilities.

When we tie our identity to something outside of ourselves such as a job, a person, a role we become attached to something other than our true identity. For example, consider these phrases:

I am a yoga teacher.

I am John's wife.

I am Mia's friend.

In these cases, we no longer practice Aparigraha (or non-attachment), the last Yama of the Yoga Sutras.

When we detach from our self-imposed "identity" and lose preconceived labels, we allow ourselves to be human — to be uniquely ourselves. We learn to accept that we are flawed as well as evolving humans with limitless potential and talent.

CHAPTER THREE

CHANGE YOUR BRAIN

"If you hear a voice within you saying, 'You cannot paint,' then by all means, paint and that voice will be silenced." — Vincent Van Gogh

I OPEN the door and a sudden thick silence permeates the air as 20 eyes are intently focused on me. I quickly scan the room for a familiar, friendly face — even one person I know — but what I see appears to be scowls, frowns, and looks of impatience. My heart races. My palms sweat. I am relieved to be wearing black yoga clothes so no one can notice the sweat. I have a lump in my throat and my hands feel like they are trembling. I hear the intro to Eminem's "Lose Yourself" in my head and think, "Please God, don't let me choke."

We've all experienced that anxious feeling — the butterflies we feel before a job interview, a public speaking engagement, or a performance. This is how I feel before I teach yoga. Not every time, but often. I have learned to sit with these nervous signals and shift their message into signals of "excitement". This hasn't been easy, but I now even look forward to getting these butterflies and I am writing to share how you too, can make nerves your friend.

. . .

Don't Believe Everything You Think

Most of the time, nerves bubble to the surface when we anticipate something going wrong. We start to lose faith that we are capable of handling mishaps. I am not suggesting you get rid of the nerves; I am suggesting that you reframe your thoughts.

We all experience nervous chatter in our head. It's the voice within that fires off automatic thoughts... some of which aren't so pleasant. If you take a moment for self-reflection, I suspect you will conclude that many of the negative thoughts are actually irrational and not reality based. These are known as distorted thoughts. They are biased beliefs that we unknowingly reinforce over time.

These patterns of thought are difficult to recognize and change. It takes practice to challenge and reframe your thoughts, but it is possible. Below are examples of common, distorted thoughts and how they may show up in yoga teacher training and beyond.

Mental Filter

When you focus only on negative aspects of a situation and filter out anything positive.

Situation: Your manager gives you feedback stating your class was well planned and you have great cues. She suggests you work on projecting your voice to keep energy high and further engage your students.

Distortion: You completely ignore the positive feedback. What you focus on and hear is that you have low energy.

Disqualifying the Positive

When you dismiss the positive feedback and decide it is not important or does not count.

Situation: A friend attends your class and tells you she enjoyed it.

Distortion: You dismiss the comment and believe that she is just saying what you want to hear because she is your friend.

EITHER/OR

When you see things in absolutes (always, never, everyone, nobody). You label everything as either/or, good or bad, black or white, success or failure.

Situation: You forgot to cue the last two postures in a sequence.

Distortion: You label yourself a failure because your sequence was not perfect.

OVER-GENERALIZING

Taking a single unpleasant event as evidence that all future events will have the same result.

Situation: You have a class and nobody shows up.

Distortion: You believe that nobody will ever show up for your class.

MIND READING

Interpreting the thoughts and beliefs of others without supporting proof.

Situation: A student leaves your class before savasana.

Distortion: You immediately believe it is because they disliked you or your class.

FORTUNE TELLING

Making a negative prediction even when there is no evidence to support its conclusion.

Situation: You have a test out (audition) coming up.

Distortion: You believe you will forget your sequence in spite of studying and being prepared.

CATASTROPHIZING

Exaggerating the importance of negative events.

Situation: A student tells you that you missed the left side of your Sun B.

Distortion: You immediately assume the student will tell your manager and you will be fired.

PERSONALIZING

Assuming responsibility for negative events that are not under your control.

Situation: A student sprains her ankle in your class.

Distortion: You say to yourself, "She would not have twisted her ankle if I cued better in class. It's my fault."

CHALLENGE YOUR THOUGHTS

There are always "what ifs" in life. These are the things that we cannot control. Even though our thoughts are automatic, we can choose whether or not to believe them and how we respond. These actions are completely within our control.

Similar to when you practice yoga and perhaps twist your body like a pretzel or stretch into a back bend that restricts your breathing, you may want to give in to the negative chatter. It takes effort to challenge those thoughts and reframe the negative and replace it with encouraging self-talk such as, "You can do this." Remind yourself, "You have faced difficult challenges in the past; you can do it again."

The same is true of your pre-class nerves. We often replay fear-based and distorted thoughts over and over. This is known as a negative thought loop. It includes:

- "I am not good enough."
- "I am going to fail."
- "I always fail."
- "This is too hard."
- "I can't do this."
- "I suck."

REFRAME YOUR THOUGHTS

Learn to replace negative self-talk with positive statements that will serve as a mantra.

"I am not good enough" becomes "I am enough!"

"I am going to fail" becomes "I will succeed!"

"I always fail" becomes "I sometimes fail, but not always."

"This is too hard" becomes "This is challenging, but I am strong."

"I can't do this" becomes "I can't, until I can!"

"I suck" becomes "Why NOT me?"

OVER TIME, REPEATED NEGATIVE THOUGHT LOOPS BECOME negative mantras. Unlike a mantra that frames your thoughts into positivity, these mantras form bad habits and become imbedded in the brain. The neuropathways that result from these thoughts become automatic and a default reaction, which can result in depression and anxiety.

Yet, the human brain is malleable, and we can change our thoughts and break negative thought patterns by making new connections in the brain. When you intercept a thought, break the loop, and replace the negative message with a positive mantra, you can form new pathways and in essence, reframe your thoughts. As mentioned before, this change in the brain is known as Neuroplasticity. Like yoga, this is a practice, and the key is repetition.

To REFRAME YOUR THOUGHTS, YOU NEED TO DO THREE things:

1. Notice the thought.
2. Challenge the thought.
3. Replace the thought.

When you have a negative thought, ask yourself for proof or evidence. Let us examine the common negative thought that often plagues new yoga teachers: "I am not good enough or capable enough to teach yoga."

How can you challenge this thought? Below are methods to do so:

TRUST

You are a trained yoga teacher. You are more capable than you give yourself credit.

PERSPECTIVE

I am completely new to this. Every teacher started off where I am now. I gain teaching experience by actually teaching.

VISUALIZE

You have undoubtedly visualized something going wrong. Now take it one step further and visualize how you successfully handle it.

. . .

Serve Your Students

Teaching is about your students. They are not there to watch you. They are there to practice yoga. When you shift your focus on how to best serve your students, the spotlight stops shining on you. This is a great way to get back to the present moment and the purpose of why you are there. Remember , you have been nervous before and survived.

Talk to Your Nerves

Welcome your nerves. Say hello. Remind yourself that nerves simply mean something is important to you. Tell your nerves that you are prepared.

Mantra

Come back to your mantra. "Its just yoga."

Believe to Achieve

Similar to creating the positive mindset that ignites Neuroplasticity, you have the ability to believe you can achieve. The belief in our ability to meet a challenge head on and complete a task successfully is called Self Efficacy. We must "believe to achieve."

Before you are able to make positive changes in your life, you have to believe you are capable. Many people confuse self-efficacy with self-esteem and self-confidence. While they are intricately linked, they are not interchangeable.

Self-efficacy is your belief that you have the power within to achieve a desired outcome. Self-esteem is based on an overall feeling of one's worth or value. While self-esteem is focused more on "being" (e.g., High self-esteem is the feeling that you are perfectly acceptable as you are), self-efficacy is focused more on "doing" (e.g., The feeling that you capable of taking on a specific task or challenge).

Self-confidence, on the other hand, is more of a certainty or assurance of self. I can feel good about who I am and still think that I am not capable to handle a task successfully.

You may feel confident and proud of who you are (self-confidence), and feel you deserve to be successful (self-esteem), BUT you do not believe you have what it takes to be a successful yoga teacher (self-efficacy).

I will never forget when I told a friend that I did not get the job with CorePower Yoga and he responded, "Well, some people are not meant to be yoga teachers." His intention was to ease my discomfort, but his statement and underestimation of my ability was just the charge I needed to prove to myself and to him, that he was wrong. Thank you ego for scoring high on the self-efficacy scale! It was my belief in my ability to achieve that motivated me to take on the challenge, audition again, and be hired.

CONFIDENCE, GET READY FOR ME

So how do you become more confident, increase self-esteem, and believe that you can achieve what you set out to do? Through his research on the topic of self-efficacy, Psychologist Albert Bandura noticed four different ways to develop self-efficacy.

1) MASTERY OF EXPERIENCES

There is no better way to believe in one's ability and launch onto the road to goal-achievement than to set a goal, persist through challenges, and enjoy satisfying results. Once a person has done this enough times (There is that repetition/practice thing again!), your belief that sustained effort and perseverance through adversity leads to success will grow.

Positive Self Talk: "I have been successful in the past. I can be successful again."

2) SOCIAL MODELING

Another way that a person can build self-efficacy is by witnessing demonstrations of competence by people who are similar to them (Bandura, 2008).

Positive Self Talk: "If she can do it, so can I." Come back to my mantra: *"Why NOT me".*

3) SOCIAL PERSUASION

When a person is told that they have what it takes to succeed, they are more likely to achieve success. A good mentor serves as a trusted voice of encouragement.

Positive Self Talk: *"She believes I can, so I should believe I can."*

4) STATES OF PHYSIOLOGY

Lastly, our emotions, moods, and physical states influence how we judge our self-efficacy (Kavanagh & Bower, 1985).

Positive Self Talk: "It is that time of the month. This feeling will pass."

Self-efficacy becomes a self-fulfilling prophecy (Eden & Zuk, 1995).

Self-confidence is the trust you have in yourself to engage successfully in the world. When you have self-confidence, you believe you are able to rise to new challenges and seize opportunities and are able to recover when things do not go as planned.

Most importantly, those who have self-confidence do not internalize their value based on what others think or on things outside of their control. They are able to make mistakes, take responsibility and move on.

So I get it, you might "understand" confidence in theory, but how do you gain more of it? Well, the truth is...you practice it. You act as if you already have it.

Courage also plays an important part in confidence. Every time you have the courage to try something you are fearful of, you build confidence.

You may have been encouraged to keep up your yoga practice, separate from your yoga teaching. The reason for this is that your yoga practice helps you build the skills needed to overcome self-doubt, manage anxiety and stress, and challenge yourself to reach beyond.

ACT As IF

When you believe you can achieve and have visualized it, you are able to re-write your script and become your very own success story. But sometimes we need to play the part and act as if, for it to become so. Again, the more you practice, the better you get.

Life is a series of choices you make. It is pretty simple in fact, when you make different choices, you reach different outcomes.

I must have been about 30-years-old when I started a Facebook profile page. In doing so, the platform asked: "What is your favorite quote?" I thought long and hard about this. I reflected about what resonated with me. One quote from Dr. Laura Schlessinger came to mind: "Act as if." I liked it, but at that moment I took it a step further and came up with my 'Why NOT me' motto, and it changed the course of my life.

Why couldn't I be the success story? Why couldn't I be the one who lost weight, got the dream job or the dream house, wrote the book, got the role in the play, or finished a marathon? Why couldn't I be the person I wanted to be — the person that people found interesting, admired, and even adored? Truth be told, I COULD, and I AM!

But to get there, I had to do some serious, internal work. First, I had to believe it. I had to believe I was worth it. I had to believe that risk equaled reward. I had to not wish it or want it; I had to do it. And so I did.

I began to act as if I was already the person I wanted to be and gradually, my brain caught up to my thoughts. I am not sure if I became the person I wanted to be or if I finally believed I was the person I wanted to be. Regardless, the outcome was improved confidence and higher self-esteem that I carry off my mat.

SELF-FULFILLING PROPHECIES

What we believe affects how we behave. Our thoughts become self-fulling prophecies. Psychologist E. Paul Torrance writes, "A person's image of the future may be a better predictor of the future attainment than his past performance." (Paul Torrance, author of 'The Importance of Falling in Love with Something' and quoted in an article within 'Gifted Child Quarterly', 1983.)

In other words, if you can see yourself being successful in your mind's eye, you begin to see all the possibilities.

CHAPTER FOUR

THE ONLY WAY IS THROUGH

I TEACH yoga in a pretty affluent area just north of Los Angeles. As such, we get our fair share of celebrities who drop in for classes. I had only been teaching a couple of weeks when I had my first celebrity encounter at the studio. The studio where I teach requires teachers to work the front desk for 30 minutes before and after class. This is an effective way to connect with students. I happened to be subbing for a popular teacher during a prime class time. And, as a new teacher, I was fumbling with the computer trying to check in a long line of students. As I was fumbling with the computer, the next student asked to purchase a water. Without looking up, I asked for his name, and he answered just like 007... "Gretzky...Wayne Gretzky." I nearly fell over. I was embarrassed that I didn't look up and immediately recognize him. I was also filled with butterflies because he was signed up for *my* Yoga Sculpt class. I was going to lead Wayne Gretzky in a fitness class!

As class started, I could not escape the knowledge that Wayne Gretzky was in my class and the fear of being judged weighed heavily on me. I became tongue tied; I stumbled on my words; and, I could not stop looking at him during class to get a sense of whether he approved of me. He left class before savasana, which only intensified my concerns.

My ego driven brain told me all the reasons he left. I entertained thoughts that the room wasn't hot enough; I was off beat; I used the wrong breath cue; I didn't know what I was doing; I'm a fraud... and on and on.

The class felt disjointed and I felt like a horrible failure. Not one person came up to me to say thank you after class, which only intensified my fears. But guess what? I did it *and* I survived!

On another day, after teaching about four or five months so not exactly "new," but still green enough to experience butterflies, I was at my front desk shift before my regular 8:30 p.m. Yoga Sculpt class. I thankfully had a few "fans" who faithfully showed up for my class each week. But just prior to my entering the studio to start class, a last minute attendee arrived... the one and only, Britany Spears.

She was accompanied by a very large, beefy man, which I assumed was her body guard. By policy standards, it was too late to check her in, but because I knew who she was...I let her in. My nerves instantly went from a 7 to now off the charts. How would I teach a class and not be distracted by the knowledge that THE Britney Spears was in attendance? She didn't have her make-up on, nor was she wearing her Catholic school-girl outfit or signature black leather pants, but I was still well aware of her celebrity status. She was donned in baggy boxer shorts and a basic bra top that you could find at Target. Her hair was tied up in a ponytail. And, although she signed in under a pseudonym, there was no denying it was Britney. Super Star presence is an understatement.

She placed her mat in the back of the room, but she was anything but inconspicuous. She walked in and out of the room a couple times to find the right set of weights.

Without a doubt, the other students notice her, but remain respectful and draw their attention inward as true yogis do. For some reason, having her in the room gave me a newfound energy and motivation to bring it. The suppressed people pleaser in me makes a grand appearance. I have a sudden need for this person's approval. I grit my teeth as the first song plays because it's "Say Something," a Justin Timberlake song, but luckily for me Britney does not express a reaction. I carry on confidently and have command of the room. Britney surprisingly is out of breath and seems to have worked up a sweat as do the rest of the students. I end up teaching one of my better classes and feel an amazing energy rush of adrenaline, which I share with the group. We all are in this together. I even throw out an encouraging, "Great job, Britney," having totally forgotten that she signed into class under a pseudonym, but she offered me a smile, signaling I was off the hook.

Later, I was surprised to see her come back to my class not once, but twice more before her two week free promotion concluded. Although she didn't sign up for a membership after the promotion ended, I was still appreciative that having her in my class turned my nerves into excitement. Facing my fear built my confidence. I reinforced my belief that I can do this yoga teaching thing. Maybe I don't suck.

PRACTICE MAKE PROGRESS

Teaching yoga is like learning anything...it gets easier the more you do it. When you first learned to drive a car, chances are you were hyper aware of everything around you. You had to consciously consider what you were doing, what you were supposed to do, what other drivers were doing, take note of obstacles on the road, where you were going, and how to get there. It's exhausting and a lot of energy is expelled.

Not to mention the smaller details one has to consciously consider: remain within the lines, the speed limit, check the rearview mirror, the right of way at a four-way stop. Do you remember that constant chatter that happened in your head while you first started driving and gripped the wheel for dear life?

But I'm willing to bet you learned to drive. The sweat dripping from your brow due to stress was many years ago. Think about what happens when you get into your car now. How is it different? The fear has vanished. You just do it. We drive unconsciously (auto pilot) and perhaps we don't pay attention as carefully as we should. We might even drive with a cup of coffee in hand, one hand on the wheel, listening to a podcast, you get the idea. There are distractions that we bring onto ourselves.

Possibly, grasping for a few nerves while driving would do us good. The same applies to teaching yoga. The nerves will not always be there, but when they are, they keep us accountable.

MANAGE YOUR EXPECTATIONS

It is unreasonable to expect that you will complete yoga teacher training and be able to walk into a yoga studio and become the next Shiva Rhea or Baron Baptiste. Becoming great at anything takes work and practice.

Think progress over perfection. This is where you utilize your yoga training and practice and apply it to your life off your mat. A common yoga intention or mantra is to "be present" or "accept where you are in this moment."

I mentioned that self-esteem is how we regard ourselves. It is how we rate ourselves as human beings, how worthy we feel we are in this moment. Generally speaking, we can think of self-esteem as the extent to which we respect ourselves. Self-esteem is what we speak to in yoga when we offer up the intention of self-care, self-love, and acceptance.

In Nathaniel Brandon's book, *The Six Pillars of Self Esteem*, he presents areas of practice to build self-esteem. I recommend his book not only because it's an excellent read, but also his "six pillars" can be applied to many common yoga themes.

He discusses living consciously, self-acceptance, responsibility, assertiveness, and living a purposeful life. I'm sure that within your own self-reflection you have found additional ideas to inspire others.

Small Improvements, Big Results

Our yoga journey has taught us that perfection is unachievable. Yet, when we take on challenges that are meaningful to us, we build our self-confidence and seek out even greater challenges. With each small improvement, we see bigger results. This doesn't happen overnight.

Consistent practice and checking in with ourselves is the path to find growth. You will grow as a student and teacher, but as you strive for growth, try to view your journey from a positive viewpoint. Instead of looking at how far you need to go, it is just as important to look at how far you have come.

CHAPTER FIVE

DISCOVER YOUR SUPERPOWER

"WHO ARE YOU?" This can be a loaded question. It is probably second to, "And what do you do?"

As you recall, the last of the Yamas in Patanjali's Eight Limbs of Yoga is Aparigraha, known as non-attachment. When we attach ourselves to an identity that is linked to a person, a profession, a social class, a talent, or an ability, we actually lose our identities. This is why I urge you to replace the statement, *I am a Yoga Teacher* to *I teach yoga.*

I used to run mental health groups for a treatment facility. One of my clients was a 28-year-old retired pro motor cross racer. He had been sponsored by a big corporate brand and was making a ton of money. Riding motor bikes was all he ever wanted to do. And then one day, he was in an accident that left him unable to return to his sport. This loss of his perceived identity brought about a serious case of depression and substance abuse along with suicidal ideation. This client could not let go of his belief and vision that without the identity of being a professional motor cross racer, he was nobody.

When you value your worth based on an identity, you will cause yourself unnecessary suffering. Instead of seeing an identity as something you ARE, think of your identity as anything you do consistently and repetitively. The collection of your daily habits and what you practice consistently are what make up your identity. This is fluid and evolving. Identities are simply roles we play. Identities are shaped by circumstance, people's expectations and hopes, and self-imposed beliefs. Your identity is a badge you wear or a costume you put on. Your identity has absolutely nothing to do with who you are or your value.

It sucks to have to re-evaluate who you think you are when you have been certain you were born to do something in particular. My motor cross client naturally needed time to grieve the loss of his identity, but this process would have been smoother had he reframed his identity as someone who races bikes professionally instead of labeling himself "a professional bike racer".

The mental shift from "I am" to "I do" frees you to reinvent yourself anytime you want, to try new things, to be open to all possibilities. This can be the most empowering thing you can ever do.

When you realize that you are an evolving person, you can harness your many superpowers. You can start to let go of needing someone else to tell you who you are. You may find that you are your own "expert" and you trust your intuition. You can even let go of the feedback you received in yoga teacher training that implied if you had "it" or "what it takes" to teach yoga. To be clear, receiving feedback is an integral part of teacher training and life. But feedback should be taken with a grain of salt and tempered to what you intuitively know and seek within your own personal challenges. Feedback is valuable input and good to take under advisement, but someone's opinion is only an opinion. You need to take feedback, reflect, and decide if it is constructive or destructive to your self-esteem.

Although teacher training can be a valuable tool for self-discovery and help challenge you to grow personally, pinning your identity to being a yoga teacher by someone else's standards can eat away at your self-esteem. Do not let someone else's feedback define who you are as a person. You are many things and do many things. Teaching yoga is only ONE of them.

At the end of this book, you will find exercises to help you look inward and determine your strengths as well as what you enjoy doing.

OVERCOME YOUR INSECURITIES

You have completed your training. You are certified. Whether you further your studies and apply what you learned to teach yoga is up to you. Just because you can, does not mean that you have to.

Any personal growth activity such as taking part in yoga teacher training, reading this book, or an exercise in self-awareness is never a waste. If you decide you do not want to teach yoga, that is okay. But realize that if you are shying away from teaching because of a fear, this can be overcome.

I conducted a survey and found that there were three areas that new yoga instructors found intimidating. The number one fear facing new yoga instructors was concern over not being competent. The second most common fear was that their students would not like their sequence. Lastly, many worried that nobody would show up for their class. All of these fears are based on not feeling confident.

Let's take a look at each of these fears and see what you can do to overcome your insecurities and bring your best to your students during each and every class.

Yoga is different things to different people. First, decide for yourself what it means to you and what you want to impart to others. The clearer you are on your purpose for teaching yoga, the better.

Among the yoga teachers that I work with all teach because they are passionate about yoga. They share a common goal of wanting to share their practice with others. But they also have unique reasons and interests for why they teach. One is interested in pre-natal yoga and wants to help pregnant women find optimum health. She even works as a doula aside from teaching yoga. Another associate is interested in sports psychology and how yoga can help pro athletes find mental focus. One friend has a dance background and wants to focus her class on the grace of movement.

For me, I want to teach students how to become more aware of the sensations in their bodies, how to listen to their inner guide, and how to get more in touch with their thoughts and emotions. There is no right or wrong. It simply is a matter of finding your purpose for teaching yoga, finding your own style and voice, and finding your niche.

CHAPTER SIX

MAKE YOUR CLASS YOUR OWN

"I've learned that people will forget what you said, people will forget what you did, but people will never forget how you made them feel." — Maya Angelou

I TEACH three very different types of yoga classes with three very different audiences. It is important to know who your students are so you can best serve them. How you deliver the message is entirely dependent on who the message is intended.

With yoga, one size does NOT fit all. I teach a heated Yoga Sculpt class, which is a fast-paced and challenging class. Someone new to yoga will likely find this class intimidating and that could easily turn them off from yoga entirely. Knowing your student will help you to guide them to an appropriate fit for a yoga class.

Most students who enjoy Sculpt have similar expectations for the class and tend to be there for its physical benefits. I have to ask myself what it is that these students need from this class. Because the nature of the class is focused on repetition and burning out muscles, I find what students need most from me is the motivation to keep going. These students demand a challenging, high energy class with lots of movement. I therefore utilize music and lighting to set a tone that will lift mood and command focus. The intentions and cues I incorporate focus on encouragement to keep my students motivated. This includes focusing on pushing limits and boundaries. My approach is to guide students away from being in their heads and focus on uplifting them and distracting them from unwanted thoughts. The focus is on lightness, fun and joy, but also on strength, power and control.

In contrast, my beginning yoga class is just that, beginning yoga. Students who are new to yoga require a completely different type of class with a completely different intention. My goal for this class is to ease students into yoga. My focus is on gentle, slow and more instructive cues. It is key for a beginner to feel safe and comfortable. Learning about postures and how to listen to your own body can be challenging.

As a teacher, you must be aware of the type of student taking your class. The beginning student may have injuries or have little fitness experience and lack strength and flexibility. They require simple and clear instructions. Beginners must feel safe and supported both physically and emotionally. For a beginner class, I focus on themes to align with this. Themes like self-acceptance and trust are appropriate for a beginner's class.

My Vinyasa Flow class is the most challenging to prepare. The students who take this class are more advanced in their physical practice. This class allows for more creativity in transitions and new ways to sequence postures that will provide variety while still challenging the students. It is equally important for me to sequence a flow that makes sense, feels good in the body, while maintaining safety. A theme that I might choose for this type of class may be strength, balance, or breath.

Knowing your audience and the class type they expect is the first step in building self-confidence and discovering why you want to be a teacher. Then, you can work to make your class your own by finding your purpose, your style, your tribe, and creating your brand.

YOUR PURPOSE

Understanding your core values will help you determine why you want to teach yoga. It will also help you narrow your yoga niche and ultimately, help you find your life purpose. The more you know about your own motivations and your own talents, the better you will be at cultivating the life you want to live. Complete the self-reflection exercises in the back of this book to help you find your purpose.

YOUR STYLE

Developing your style as a teacher will come naturally with practice. As long as you remain authentic and teach from your heart, you will find students who will be naturally and organically drawn to you. Not all students will like your style and that is okay. You have heard the phrase, "You can't please all the people all the time," and that could not be truer than with teaching yoga. Remember my earlier analogy... not everyone loves peaches!

Are you worried because your classes are empty? Try not to take it personally. Before allowing negative thoughts to creep into your psyche, such as *I am an awful teacher* or *everyone hates me*, challenge your ego and consider all the possibilities for why you are not drawing people to your class.

It took me a long time to get over the fact that some people simply don't care for me. Maybe I remind them of someone else, or they see things in me that they do not like in themselves. Whatever the reason, I needed to let those thoughts go. Trust me. You will find your people and your people will find you. You just need to know where to look and be patient. Know that with a little perseverance and some targeted marketing, you will develop your own following over time.

Your Tribe

Take a moment to look at the classes you take. Why do you gravitate toward a class? Does the time fit into your schedule? Do you make room in your schedule for a certain teacher's class? Do you feel a kinship with the other students who take the class? These are important things to think about when you question why someone is or is not taking your class.

Get to know your students. Who you want in your class is less important than who actually comes to your class. Have you ever asked for specific feedback? Ask your students what they like about your class. Learn your students' names, but also learn something about who they are. I suggest getting contact information emails and phone numbers so that even if you leave your studio job, you have a direct connection to your students.

You can always consider planning a special event and inviting your regular students or simply keep the connection open with a newsletter or a random check-in if they have missed class just to see if they are okay. These are small gestures and acts of kindness, but they also help build and strengthen the student-teacher relationship.

Your Brand

Anybody can give basic cues and develop a sequence, but nobody can teach like you. Once you can recognize your unique attributes and what makes you different from other yoga teachers, you can begin to reach out to students who will be most attracted to the way you teach and who you are. This is what personal branding is all about.

Personal branding begins with a bio. A bio is a brief summary about you. A yoga bio is a brief summary about you as a yoga teacher. Your yoga bio will list your experience and give the reader an overview about who you are and what to expect from your class. Consider including the following:

YOUR TRAINING AND EXPERIENCE

Do you have any specialized training or have you studied a particular style of yoga? Include other relevant work experience and studies that may enhance your yoga teaching. Do you have a background in ballet or gymnastics? Do you have any certifications in personal training, body work or massage therapy that may give you a unique perspective of the mind/body connection?

YOUR CLASS FORMAT AND STYLE

What should students expect when they walk into your class? A high five? A great big hug? A joke? Maybe they know you will call them out and they are ready to impress. Maybe your students know they will be able to feel like they can escape and turn inward with no pressure to engage in a smile. Are you an adjuster and your students look forward to some hands-on assistance? Are you going to play some hip hop or keep the lights turned down low?

YOUR PERSONALITY

Students not only want to know what to expect from your class, but also what they to expect from you. There is no need to embellish, exaggerate, or try to impress. You want your yoga bio to be accurate and true to you. If you are reading this book, you are probably still trying to figure this out for yourself. Use the exercises to look inward so you can be crystal clear on who you are and what you can offer your students.

· · ·

EXTRAS

You might also want to include details about prominent yoga teachers who and/or styles that have influenced you. You could also include a section on your approach to yoga. What do you hope to achieve every time you come to your mat?

Even if nobody sees your bio, the exercise of writing it forces you to narrow your focus and be clear on your teaching style.

CHAPTER SEVEN

ATTRACT A LOYAL FOLLOWING

WITHOUT A DOUBT, yoga is a healing practice. Yoga not only fosters a healthy body, but also, a healthy mind. When you link breath to movement in a vinyasa style class, something magical happens when a group of people flow together. The simple act of moving as one and breathing as one, connects us as one.

When you are the teacher who leads this effort, you will find that students come back to you time and time again. Finding your ideal student — the ones who connect with your personal style of teaching yoga — will result in a rewarding experience for yourself and the others who take your class.

Let's discuss how to attract your students and give them the best class ever.

YOUR IDEAL STUDENT

If you are already teaching, take note of who returns to your class. Ask for feedback. Find out what your students like or in some cases, what they would like less of. Discover where they feel changes could benefit the class experience. You don't have to necessarily adapt your class to one person, but if you hear the same feedback regularly then you know that a change might be in order. When you know your students' preferences, you can start to determine how to structure your class to target your ideal student.

STRUCTURING A CLASS

There are infinite ways to structure a yoga class. So where do you begin?

1. Know your student. Find out what they need.
2. Find your niche by combining your student audience with their need.
3. Build a sequence. Keep it simple. Build a framework and adjust as needed. Prepare, plan, but stay flexible.
4. Know yourself. Be clear on what you have to offer.
5. Serve your students. Keep your students safe and meet them where they are.

We already talked a little about how to know who you are and the importance of knowing your student. Let's talk more about #3 above, Building a sequence.

GROUPING BUCKETS

There are more than 1,000 different choices of yoga postures that can be incorporated into class. Realistically, you will probably use 20-30 different postures in a 60-minute class and many of these will be repeated on both sides and repeated multiple times during class (think Downward Dog or Crescent Lunge).

Of course, you would never be expected to know every yoga pose in the world. Instead, work on slowly building your memory bank of poses over time.

As I will explain later in the chapter, when you are start out as a new teacher, it makes the most sense to work with a template class and simply vary it.

For the first few classes you teach, you may over-prepare by planning out alternative postures you might add into your flow if you end up with extra time. After a while, you will be able to walk into a room and make adjustments on the fly. For now, it is most important to focus on building up your confidence.

Before I dive into how to sequence, it is helpful if you study individual postures and learn more about how they are grouped. Pick a posture and first see what grouping it falls into (standing, balancing, supine, prone, etc.). For example:

- Standing Poses: Mountain, Chair
- Supine Poses (on your back): Bridge, Happy Baby
- Prone Poses (belly down): Cobra, Floor Bow, Locust

Next, see all the different variations you can make with it. This will help you to offer modifications and up levels to your students. This is where a software like Tummee Yoga Sequence Builder, Pocket Yoga Teacher App or Mark Stephen's Yoga Sequencing flash cards can be handy.

There are many different layers of yoga and infinite ways to teach a class. I liken it to how a musician approaches writing a piece of music. A musician can focus on the lyrics, the melody, a specific instrument, or vocal tone. But a musician cannot do it all at once, nor would we want him/her to. A musician usually has a style, but each work can have a different focus and sound. Once you get your style down, you can then play around with a different emphasis.

Even the same song can be performed infinite ways. It is the same with a yoga sequence. By making minor changes to one sequence, you can have a completely different effect on the listener/student.

It is alright to search for online resources to find sequencing ideas and ways to build a sequence. Fortunately, there are many options from YouTube to the software I mention above. Try not to get overwhelmed with the many options available.

Keep It Simple

My biggest piece of advice for you as a new teacher is to keep your sequence simple. Until you are clear on your teaching style or niche and who your ideal students are, the best rule of thumb is to keep it simple and work on your confidence through practice.

A good target is to keep your sequence 80% the same each time, while changing just 20% each week. Students like to know what to expect. If you know that your students are all advanced and push themselves to their limits, you can cater your class specific to this population. Michelle Berman Marchildon touches on this in her book, *Theme Weaver*. She recalls advice she received as a new teacher: teach the same sequence for about 25 classes.

The idea behind this suggestion is that when you teach the same sequence repeatedly, it will be committed to memory. This will not only help you build confidence, but it will also free you up to refine your teaching style to work in themes.

As a new teacher, who is finding their niche, keep your postures and sequence simple enough to appeal to a broad audience. Aim for a base sequence that allows beginners to modify poses, but also allows advanced yogis to level up.

Once you get your confidence legs and you have practiced a hell of a lot, you will be able to determine your unique teaching style and your strengths. Growing your class and refining the details will come organically.

CHAPTER EIGHT

MEET EXPECTATIONS & SEQUENCE WITH CONFIDENCE

THERE ARE infinite choices of music, postures, and cues available to you. No doubt, it can be overwhelming. In order to meet your students' expectations and deliver a class that hits the mark time and time again, remember my advice from the previous chapter... keep it simple.

1. Pick a base sequencing template.
2. Select a few postures for each grouping.
3. Teach a lot.

BUILDING A SEQUENCE

No two yoga classes are ever the same. The way I learned to build a sequence and what I find works, is to start with a framework and add layers from there. You will make your class your own, but having a solid foundation is a good starting point.

I was taught to break up the class into chunks. CorePower Yoga calls them buckets. Other teacher trainings may call them blocks. This is how some teachers structure a class that makes sense. Poses are combined in small groupings to make sequencing a whole lot easier.

SAMPLE CLASS SEQUENCE
Intention
Starting Pose
Warm-up
Sun A
Sun B
Standing Poses
Seated Poses
Core and Spine Work
Balancing
Cool Down
Surrender

SEQUENCING MAY INCLUDE ONE OF THE FOLLOWING approaches:

Peak Posture – Building a sequence of postures leading up to a peak posture.

Layer Sequence – A layer sequence is a style of class where you start with a base posture or flow and then add on to it. For example, the first layer could be a flow ending in Warrior Two. The next layer, you would follow Warrior Two with another pose, perhaps Reverse Triangle. The third flow, you would add on one more layer... Warrior Two, Reverse Triangle followed by Extended Side Angle. You can teach a layer flow for an entire hour and only have to incorporate a few additional postures.

One Slow, 2 Flow – A flow that is repeated on both sides. The first flow is cued slowly for set up and the postures are held for a few breaths. The flow is then repeated one breath to one movement two more times.

Block Sequence – A series of poses that move from one block to another. Each block includes postures from the same grouping. One block may be a standing series, another a balancing series, and even a core series. CorePower Yoga sequences in this manner. Sample Balancing block: Eagle to Tree to Dancer's; Sample Prone Spine Strengthening block: Cobra to Locus to Floor Bow.

Linear - Moving from one posture to the next, advancing in complexity and challenge from beginning of the sequence to the end. Postures typically are not repeated.

MANY BOOKS HAVE BEEN WRITTEN ON YOGA SEQUENCING. I will reference some that you might be interested in to dive deeper into sequencing and creative transitioning at the end of the book. For now, I will focus on sequencing for the new teacher who wants to gain confidence.

It doesn't matter what approach you start with. Just pick one and stay with it. Keep it simple!

CLASS STRUCTURE BREAKDOWN

Whatever type of sequence approach you choose, you will want to include the basics.

BASIC FRAMEWORK FOR POWER YOGA CLASS

Grounding Posture / Starter

This is your initial starting pose of class. It is used to ground the student. This is a good time to connect the student with their breath and include some guided visualization and/or intention setting. It is a good idea to stay in this posture for a few breaths to give students a chance to set their focus and connect with the present moment.

Examples are:

- Seated (easy pose)
- Standing (standing at attention)
- Prone (child's pose)
- Supine (savasana, butterfly, etc.)

Warm Up

Something that opens the spine: front/back (forward folds and backbends), side/side (side bends), right/left (twists). Some examples of spine warm-ups:

. . .

SEATED

Seated side bends

Seated twists

Seated forward folds

STANDING

Standing side bends

Small back bends (avoid intense back bends during warm up)

Cactus arms to each side

Sunflowers

BELLY DOWN

Table Top

Cat/Cow

Thread the Needle

Bird Dog with elbow to knee

Rag Doll

HEAT BUILDING POSTURES (SUN SALUTATIONS)

Sun A is a basic set of postures that typically involve moving from mountain pose and ending in a downward facing dog. Depending on the style of practice, Sun A typically is around 5-12 postures. (I suggest creating 3-5 different Sun A sequences that you can switch out).

One example is: mountain, forward fold, halfway lift, chaturanga (high plank, low plank, upward facing dog, downward facing dog).

Sun B (continues to build heat in the body and also begins to bring in strength building). This is the "meat of class".

I suggest creating 5-10 different mini flow sequences. My sample mini flows include: crescent series, warrior series, fallen star, horizon lunge, standing splits.

Then, it's nice to break it up in the middle of class to give students a chance to catch their breath, drink water, and towel off. It's also a chance to give their legs a break from standing and move onto a core workout.

Core workouts don't have to be limited to sit ups. Boat postures can offer a challenging core workout and be varied with arm and foot placement. Holding planks or forearm planks offer a core workout and serve as a break because they continue to build strength with low risk of injury.

It is also nice to add a little play time in the middle of class to allow students a chance to listen to what their bodies need and practice postures. Play time can be guided or simply free time allowing students a chance to explore postures on their own.

If you are using an inversion as your peak "ta-dah" posture, you can demo a modified version so that students can practice during free time. This break serves as a reset. From here you can work on more balancing postures and other challenging postures in your Sun C flow.

STRENGTHENING AND BALANCING POSTURES (SUN C)

In the Power Yoga style I practice and teach, Sun C is often another standing series and introduces more advanced balancing moves and works students toward the peak posture. Because students are adequately open and warmed by this point, this series of postures typically involves fewer poses but longer holds.

You should always balance your peak posture with a counter posture. If you do a huge heart opener like wheel, find a neutral posture like bound angle pose or fallen bridge before cuing for a counter posture like a forward fold. This neutral posture is important to rest and re-set the body.

After Sun C, you can use this as another break period to add in more core work, spine strengthening or seated postures. Other options include having students lie on their back for bridge, legs up the wall, or plow pose to begin the cool down.

COOL DOWN

As students cool down, the body calls for supine postures, lying on one's back and utilizing gravity for release and surrender. Some great postures for this include happy baby, supine twists, or supine figure four. Always end your class with savasana for a minimum of two minutes to allow the body to absorb the benefits of their practice.

PLANNING YOUR SEQUENCE

- Step 1: Pick a peak posture.
- Step 2: Pick a starting pose. Determine what muscles need to be open to safely achieve the peak posture.
- Step 3: Pick three spinal warm ups. Ensure you include all planes of the body.
- Step 4: Pick a Sun A flow.
- Step 5: Select 2-3 Sun B mini flows that will utilize muscles for the peak posture.
- Step 6: Add a core and balancing section.
- Step 7: Create a Sun C flow that incorporates your peak. You can use an existing mini block flow and incorporate the peak pose within the flow.
- Step 8: Pick a counter posture.
- Step 9: Select cool down postures that will allow for gentle stretching and release of muscles.

To keep things simple, it is totally fine and in many cases better to keep the same postures for your starting, warming, core and cooling blocks and to simply vary your Sun B and C. Trust me, this will take an immense amount of pressure off you when planning your sequences. It allows you to really get the teaching experience and confidence you need under control. The rest will come with time.

CHAPTER NINE

BUILDING UPON YOUR BASE SEQUENCE

ONCE YOU HAVE the basics down of creating your class structure including an intention, your peak posture, and how to lead up to it, you can build upon a base sequence using a block method. I've included templates in this chapter to show you how simple, yet effective this method can be in creating a class that is satisfying and meets various student levels.

BUILDING WITH BLOCKS

Blocks are a series of postures grouped together. Below is an example of how you can go about grouping postures.

- Standing Poses
- Seated Postures
- Balancing Postures
- Supine Postures (on your back)
- Prone Postures (belly down)
- Core Postures
- Forward Bends
- Inversions

- Arm Balancing

When you sequence using blocks, you move from one block of postures (standing) to another (balancing). Blocks are easier to sequence when you are first starting out because you can begin with a basic block framework template and simply change the postures within each block.

For instance, a balancing block may include the poses eagle, then tree, followed by dancer's. You can change this balancing block easily by starting with eagle, moving to airplane, and then warrior 3.

As you can see in the sample blocks that follow, the three postures that are grouped together are all balancing postures. The only thing that has changed is which balancing postures are selected.

Keep in mind, there is no rule to sequencing. If you use blocks, feel free to mix up your blocks and repeat them. For example, you can choose to do a standing block then a core block and back to a standing block followed by a balancing block.

As you study the two examples of sample blocks that follow, try to think of a third example for your own sequencing.

BALANCING BLOCK #1	BALANCING BLOCK #2
EAGLE	EAGLE
DANCERS	AIRPLANE
TREE	WARRIOR 3

PRONE BLOCK #1	PRONE BLOCK #2
COBRA	SPHINX
LOCUST	PUPPY DOG POSE
FLOOR BOW	CHILD'S POSE

CORE BLOCK#1	CORE BLOCK#2
SIT UPS	HIP LIFTS
YOGI BICYCLES	CLAM SHELL SIT UPS
BOAT TWISTS	CLIMB THE ROPE

SEATED BLOCK #1	SEATED BLOCK#2
SEPARATE LEG SIDE STRETCH	FIRE LOG
SEATED FORWARD FOLD	LORD OF THE FISHES
REVERSE PLANK	SEATED FORWARD FOLD

SUPINE BLOCK #1	SUPINE BLOCK #2
BRIDGE (ACTIVE)	SUPINE BIG TOE POSE (ACTIVE)
SUPINE BUTTERFLY (NEUTRAL)	KNEES TO NOSE (NEUTRAL)
CHILD'S POSE (COUNTER)	SUPINE TWIST (COUNTER)

MINI FLOW BLOCKS

A "mini flow block" is when you take a group of postures from different groupings and create a mini flow, putting them together in their own mini sequence. You may sequence a balancing posture to a supine posture and back to a balancing posture.

A sample may be chair to squat and curl to boat to side plank. You can see how different types of postures are put together. The combinations are infinite. Vinyasa and Power style classes typically follow this sequencing style. This type of sequencing offers more variety, is more dynamic, and can allow for more creativity.

The downside is that it can be more challenging for students to follow. For teachers, it can be challenging to choreograph a sequence that makes sense, has safe transitions, and can be cued clearly and accurately.

However, if you create these mini sequences, you can give them a name or shorthand symbol to help you with recall. The more familiar you are with your mini sequences, the better you will be at cuing your students through safe transitions.

Your mini flow blocks can be as long or as short as you like, but typically 4-8 postures make up a block that is easy to remember. The good thing about using mini flow blocks is that you can always use them as a base and then add some variation to keep it fresh.

The mini flows pictured are examples of postures that are sequenced to work together. I gave them a name to help identify them as an example of how I commit them to memory. You can use my system or find another that works for you.

As you consistently commit your mini blocks to memory, you will be able to eventually switch it up and add some arm variations and up level on the fly.

CRESCENT BLOCK

Inhale CRESCENT LUNGE

Exhale REVOLVED CRESCENT LUNGE

Inhale EXAULTED WARRIOR

Exhale WARRIOR 2

Inhale REVERSE WARRIOR

WARRIOR BLOCK

Inhale WARRIOR 1

Exhale WARRIOR 2

Inhale RERVERSE WARRIOR

Exhale EXTENDED SIDE ANGLE

Inhale REVERSE TRIANGLE

Exhale CHATURANGA

FIG 4 STANDING BLOCK

Inhale ONE LEGGED MOUNTAIN

Exhale STANDING FIGURE FOUR

Inhale ONE LEGGED MOUNTAIN

Exhale DANCER'S POSE

Inhale MOUNTAIN POSE

Exhale FORWARD FOLD

HORIZON LUNGE BLOCK

Inhale RIGHT LEG HIGH

Exhale LOW LUNGE

Inhale RIGHT ARM HIGH

Exhale HORIZON LUNGE

Inhale SIDE PLANK

Exhale CHATURANGA

FALLEN STAR BLOCK

Inhale RIGHT LEG HIGH

Exhale KNEE TO LEFT TRICEP

Inhale FALLEN STAR

Exhale LEFT PALM DOWN

Inhale RIGHT LEG HIGH

Exhale DOWNWARD DOG

TRIANGE BLOCK

Inhale WARRIOR 2

Exhale TRIANGLE

Inhale REVERSE TRIANGLE

Exhale WARRIOR 2

Inhale STAR POSE

Exhale WIDE LEGGED FORWARD

CRESCENT MOON SPLIT
Inhale CRESCENT MOON
Exhale HALF SPLIT
Inhale STANDING SPLIT
Exhale SHIVA SQUAT
Inhale STANDING SPLIT
Exhale LOW LUNGE

CACTUS REVOLVED
Inhale CHAIR
Exhale CHAIR PLANE
Inhale LEFT LEG MOUNTAIN
Exhale CACTUS ARM TO RIGHT
Inhale LEFT LEG MOUNTAIN
Exhale LOW FLYING CRESCENT

DOWNDOG WINDSHIELD
Inhale RIGHT LEG HIGH
Exhale KNEE TO RIGHT TRICEP
Inhale RIGHT LEG HIGH
Exhale KNEE TO LEFT TRICEP
Inhale RIGHT LEG HIGH
Exhale LOW LUNGE

RUNNER'S LUNGE
Inhale CRESCENT LUNGE
Exhale REVOLED CRESCENT
Inhale FLY YOUR ARMS
Exhale RUNNER'S LUNGE
Inhale SIDE PLANK
Exhale CHATURANGA

CHAIR TO CRESCENT
Inhale CHAIR
Exhale PRAYER TWIST TO THE RIGHT
Inhale HOVER YOUR LEFT FOOT
Exhale REVOLVED CRESCENT
Inhale CRESCENT LUNGE
Exhale WARRIOR 2

CRESCENT STAR
Inhale CRESCENT LUNGE
Exhale DOUBLE LUNGE
Inhale CRESCENT LUNGE
Exhale WARRIOR 2
Inhale STAR POSE
Exhale WIDE LEGGED FORWARD

PUTTING IT TOGETHER EXERCISE

Let's look at how to put a mini flow block together. Start with a base posture and think of 5 different options for the next posture.

Keep going from there. Your second posture will now be your

base. Let's look at the example of starting your base pose with "inhale chair." Next, you have options including:

- Inhale chair; exhale prayer twist; or
- Inhale chair; exhale interlace your fingers behind your back; or
- Inhale chair; exhale airplane your arms; or
- Inhale chair; exhale forward fold; or
- Inhale chair; exhale eagle

Your second posture is now your base where you continue. If you chose "exhale prayer twist", where could you go next? Remember the breath will be an inhale.

- Exhale prayer twist; inhale chair; or
- Exhale prayer twist; inhale exalted warrior; or
- Exhale prayer twist; inhale hover your right foot; exhale revolved crescent; or
- Exhale prayer twist; inhale left leg mountain

Let's try another one with your base posture being extended side angle. From extended side angle, where can you go next? Some ideas:

- Reverse Warrior
- Reverse Triangle
- Triangle
- Star Pose
- W2
- Half Moon
- Low Lunge

If you think logically about the postures and each transition to go safely from one to the next, you can easily create your mini flows. With the base of extended side angle, you can also incorporate arm balances.

For example, from extended side angle, you can cue:

- Option to extend your arms overhead and reach.
- Imagine you are reaching for a beach ball.
- Option for a half bind.

Then, you can move onto a second posture like reverse warrior or star.

CHAPTER TEN

ADVANCED SEQUENCING

AS I MENTIONED, there are infinite ways to structure your class. For simplicity, once you have a handful of mini flows, you can start to build upon them. Maybe you repeat your flow and add on, but you may also include an additional posture or arm variation to the second round and another posture for your third round.

ADD ONS

Here are some add on options to make your flow more challenging for the advanced student:

Add a Sun A between blocks.

Add a different arm variation for variety. Options include:

- Eagle Arms
- T out your Arms
- Airplane your Arm
- Twists and Binds
- Hands in Prayer
- Cactus Arms
- Bound Arms

Add pulses or a static hold for a few breaths to allow students to deepen into the posture and increase their heart rate.

INCORPORATING PROPS

Using props in your yoga class is an individual choice. A prop is anything that assists a student in achieving a posture. Props may include straps, yoga blocks, bolsters, and even walls.

I have found props to be one of the most useful tools to cue students for safety, alignment, and proper form. Props are not solely utilized for modifying postures. Props can also help you deepen into a pose. If you use props in your class, make sure that you have enough for everyone. Walking students through a pose utilizing props and demoing allows them to see the versatility and benefit of their use rather than view them as a crutch. Props can be incredibly useful for all levels of practice.

WORKING WITH A PEAK POSTURE

The idea behind sequencing toward a peak posture is to create a class that revolves around that posture — the peak of class — or what I like to think of as a final hoorah! All other postures lead up to this by building required muscle strength, warming muscles, and opening muscles so that the peak posture can be achieved safely and successfully.

Make sure your peak posture is appropriate for the level of class. Your goal is for most students to attempt it. Always offer a modification. The other option is to make the modification the peak and offer the up level for more advanced students.

It's important to know that you can use a basic posture such as downward facing dog or chair pose as a peak posture. Another option is to build the entire class around an intention or theme.

. . .

SAMPLE PEAK POSTURES BASED ON LEVEL:

Beginner:

- Mountain
- Chair
- Rag Doll
- Plank
- Warrior 1
- Warrior 2

Advanced Beginners:

- Crow Pose
- Dancer's Pose
- Half Moon
- Side Plank
- Camel

Intermediate:

- Revolved Half Moon
- Side Plank with Tree leg
- Wheel
- Big Toe Pose

Advanced:

- Side Crow
- Bird of Paradise
- Full Splits

Peak postures require you to warm the student up. To sequence around a peak posture, visualize the peak posture and break it down. You can consult with other teachers or do a quick google search for prep poses leading to your peak. You should be able to answer the following questions when working with a peak posture.

- What muscles are being worked?
- What other postures will help open up these muscles?
- What is the challenging aspect of this pose?
- How can I cue to help ease students into the posture?
- How can I break the peak down in steps?

For example, consider the peak pose of *revolved half moon* and these preparation poses:

- Revolved Crescent (The twist in the thoracic spine is the same motion.)
- Extended Side Angle (Great starting base since the foot and hip placement are already in proper alignment.)
- Half Moon (Works on balance of the foot.)
- Twisted Pyramid (The placement of the hands are in the identical position needed for revolved half moon.)

A LAYERED FLOW CAN WORK WELL WITH PEAK POSTURE sequencing because each layer can build your student one step closer to the peak posture.

Next you'll find a template of a well-rounded, 60-minute class. You can see how I use mini blocks with some add-ons in my Sun B.

INTENTION

HUMILITY

"I am humble enough to know I'm not better than anyone else, but wise enough to know I am different."

PEAK

Humble Warrior

STARTING POSE

EASY SEAT

SPINAL WARM UP

Seated Side Bend
Neck Rotations
Table Top
Cat / Cow
Downward Dog
Rag Doll

SUN A
1 time slow/ 2 flow

I-Mountain
E- Forward Fold
I- Halfway Lift
E- CHATURANGA
High Plank
Low Plank
Upward Dog
Downward Dog

CHATURANGA

SUN B
1 time slow /2 flow

I-Mountain
E-Baby Back Bend
I- Mountain
E- Forward Fold
I- Halfway Lift
E- High Plank
I- Cobra
E- lower down
I- High Plank
E- Downward Dog

I-Right Leg High
E-Knee to Nose
I-Right Leg High
E-Low Lunge
I-Crescent
E-Airplane Arms
I-Crescent
E-Revolved Crescent
I-Exalted Warrior

I-Reverse Warrior
E-Extended Side Angle
I-Half Moon
E-Warrior 2
I– Star
E– Horse
Pulses in Horse
I-Star
Exhale Warrior 2
I– Reverse Triangle
E– Chaturanga

BREAK
Sit Ups
Yogi Bicycles
Boat with Russian Twist
Frog Squat
Flying Frog
Child's Pose

SUN C

I—Chair
E-Airplane your Arms
I-Chair
E-Eagle on the Right
I-Right Leg Mountain
E-Dancer's Pose
I-Mountain
E-Baby Back Bend
I-Mountain
E-Forward Fold
I-Half way Lift
E-Step Left Foot back Low Lunge
I-Warrior 1
E-Humble Warrior
I-Warrior 1
E-Forward Fold
I-Halfway Lift
E-Chaturanga

Cool Down
I– Right Leg High
E- Half pigeon
I– Right Leg High
E-Downward Dog
Step Through to Seated Position
Bridge or Wheel x4
Happy Baby
Supine Twist
Tiny Ball

SAVASANA

MANDALAS

A Mandala flow is a sequence that works in a circular pattern.

You may have been in a class and find that you are facing the front, short edge of your mat and then you work your way to the back of your mat before turning back around. Sometimes you will make your way in a half circle and return back to the front and other times the sequence will have you face all sides of your mat. Mandalas add fun and creativity to your flows allowing you to "work the room". As a beginner, mandalas can be tricky to coordinate. Transitioning and remembering what leg you are on can be challenging.

There are a few key things to think about and consider when sequencing a mandala flow.

1. Decide if you want to do a half mandala (front, one side, back, same side, front) or a full mandala (front, one side, back, other side, front) around the room.

2. In order to make it all the way around the mat in one sequence, you will need to switch legs when you are at the back of your mat. Otherwise, you will end up facing the same side and doing half a mandala.

3. If you do a half mandala and then switch legs at the front of your mat to repeat the sequence on your opposite leg, this can get complicated very quickly, especially if you are repeating the sequence breath to movement. You will be alternating the sides of your mat six times! This is fine to do, but make sure it is intentional.

4. If you choose to incorporate a mandala for Sun B, I suggest you keep the flow short and simple or skip it for Sun B and incorporate a mandala for your Sun C.

Some pose options to switch legs at the back of your mat include:

- Chair and switch legs
- Downward Facing Dog and switch legs
- One legged Mountain, Chair Plane, switch legs
- Leg Kick ups to switch legs

INVERSIONS

Inversions are interesting because they are any posture where your head is below your heart. This can include a resting pose such as downward facing dog or a pose that increases your heart rate such as a handstand. Obviously these two postures are quite different from each other. Downward Facing Dog and wide leg forward fold ignite our parasympathetic system and are calming postures. They work to help calm the nervous system and can be longer holds.

Active inversions that elevate your heart rate such as headstands and handstands should not be held for lengthy periods of time as this causes compression in the vertebrae, which can lead to potential eye problems and heart complications due to a drop in blood pressure and an increase in heart rate.

The benefits of inversions may include:

- An ego boost. Inversions are one of those postures you need to build up to. Mastering something you have been working toward is very rewarding.
- Improve circulation in the body. The use of gravity provides the brain and glands with more oxygen.
- Improve your immunity. Going upside down allows lymph to more efficiently travel toward your heart. This is important because lymph is responsible for removing toxins from our cells and flushing waste and fluids from our blood vessels helping to build immunity.
- Improve energy. Because you are upside down and your head is below your heart, handstands and headstands will get blood flowing differently to the brain.
- Improve calm and relaxation. While some inversions can energize, some inversions such as shoulder stand,

plough, legs up the wall, and wide legged forward fold trigger the vagus nerve, which activates your parasympathetic system and produces feelings of balance and calm within the body.

- Flips your perspective.
- Decrease anxiety. When we go upside down and get blood pumping to the brain, serotonin levels rise and help regulate mood.

Be mindful of your students' capabilities before introducing any advanced inversions into class. If someone is injured while attempting an inversion, the consequences can be quite severe. I suggest leaving headstands and handstands out of your sequences altogether when you are starting out.

TRANSITIONS

Have you ever been in a class and the flow... well... did not flow? Maybe the teacher linked several postures together on the same leg causing your leg to shake? Maybe the transition from one posture to another was choppy and you found you needed to support yourself with another hand or come back to a neutral posture before moving into the next. Maybe you were being guided from standing to being on your back and then back up again and you felt nauseous. Maybe you were not sure exactly what you were supposed to be doing. Or, perhaps the cues did not seem to make sense for the leg or side you were on and you had to keep looking to other students for clarification.

Transitions are the way you move from one posture to another. Smooth and logical transitions ensure that your students are safe and can follow the flow.

Beware of reckless transitions. Smart sequencing always means safety first. According to Mark Stephens, author of *Yoga Sequencing*, one of the most common times yogis get injured in a yoga practice is during a transition. Transitions are the glue that gracefully and thoughtfully move you from one posture to another and move you from one block or mini flow to another.

When transitioning from one balancing posture to another, make sure that your supporting leg does not change. For example, moving from Tree pose to Warrior 3 is safe because the standing leg does not change positions. What is not safe is moving from an internal to external hip movement. Warrior 3 to half moon pose, for example, can be unsafe, as it puts a lot of strain on the standing hip and SI joint.

Be mindful of transitions and the logic of the postures. For instance, it would not make sense to go directly from side plank to a prayer twist.

Ask yourself how can you get from side plank to prayer twist safely? There are many, but here is one transition:

- Side Plank
- Plank
- Downward Dog

Now if you are in a downward dog, you can transition as follows:

- Inhale gaze forward
- Exhale jump, step or float to the top of your mat
- Inhale halfway lift
- Exhale forward fold

Here are options to continue from forward fold:

- Inhale chair
- Exhale prayer twist

The transition listed above is a common way to get from downward dog to the top of your mat and into a neutral forward fold. You can even think of it as a mini flow and call it a transition when you are writing your sequence.

All transitions should have a purpose and make sense. Additionally, try to find graceful transitions. It is difficult to switch the direction of your feet in a transition. Coming back to a neutral position before making a change in foot placement will help with flow, but more importantly, it helps keep your students safe. Consider these additional suggestions for safety:

- Understand the postures (foot placement, muscles engaged, bones involved, joints affected, flexion or extension, breath needed).
- Understand one posture's relationship to another.
- Do not be afraid of long silences between postures. Students like to have time to process the posture. Give them some room to do this by adding some space between cueing.
- Link postures with the same hip placement. An easy way to do this is to think about short edge of mat postures versus long edge of mat postures and keep those postures linked together.
- Come back to a neutral pose before switching directions or be crystal clear with slow, detailed cues through the transition.
- Short Edge: Crescents with Warrior 1 or Warrior 3.
- Long Edge: Warrior 2, Side Angle, Triangle.
- Neutral: Mountain, Downward Facing Dog, Forward Fold, Table Top, Halfway Lift

Use an additional breath between tricky transitions to signal to the student to prepare for an upcoming change in posture. Some examples of using breath to cue during a transition are below:

- Inhale your hands to heart center.
- Inhale interlace your hands behind your back.
- Inhale, shift your weight onto your right foot.
- Place your right palm on the pinky side of your left foot.
- Ground down through your left palm.
- Bend your front knee.
- Gently step your left foot back.

Tell your students what to expect for a transition:

- Demo the transition before class
- Use cues like "big move here" or "prepare for the transition".

SEQUENCES THAT MAKE SENSE

Have you ever taken a class and when it was over, something didn't seem to feel right? You might not be able to put a finger on it.

Perhaps there are environmental conditions to consider that may not be obvious to you as a new teacher. These include:

- Time Of Day

In morning classes you will find that students tend to be stiffer. Muscles are tight and will take more time to open up. It is important to slowly build up heat in the body. Maybe hold postures longer. Concentration and balance might be off as students are slowly waking up. Keep sequences less complicated.

At the end of day it is often better to work on release of tension. You can start off a little faster with flows or more challenging holds and then taper off to conclude with a longer surrender. Chances are students have been sitting at a desk or in a car for a long period of time and are eager to move in class.

- Seasons/External Forces

It's good to consider the season and set intentions that match the mood. Rainy days may call for more nurturing postures drawing attention more inward. Summer time can be a great time to incorporate themes and intentions that are fun and invite more openness and freedom in your class.

Similarly, prominent events taking place in the news or external events beyond our control may lead you to focus on intentions such as "being present", "let go of attachment", "go with the flow".

SEQUENCING TIPS

When starting out, stick with one basic sequence framework. See my templates. Become intimately comfortable with your basic framework. Do not be concerned with making it complex or getting too creative with transitions. Do not worry that you may bore your students. Students like to know what to expect and you can vary the class with music and slight changes in the sequence order or switching out an arm variation.

Be more concerned about your students being able to follow your cues or if they look confused or cannot hear you. It is not about you. It is about them receiving the message.

IN THE BEGINNING OF YOUR TEACHING JOURNEY...

- Focus on the fundamentals. Do not try to teach what you like to take; you are not there yet.
- Keep it simple.

- Focus on getting your cuing down and speaking to the body.
- Time your playlist. One strategy is to time your yoga playlist so that by the time you get to a certain song on the playlist, you know where in your flow you should be. If you're not there by the time the song comes on, you'll know you need to speed up or slow down.
- Feel free to skip things. You're the only one who knows what was in the sequence you planned.
- Build your class. Avoid going too hard or too fast. Warm up. Find the arc.

The more you teach, the more you will understand your own pace of teaching and how long a class takes. It is like driving a car. After you have been driving for awhile, you no longer need to "think" about how long you have to stop before a light. You will naturally feel the flow of your class.

SAVASANA

Imagine you've spent an entire class cuing students to be mindful and focus their attention on the present moment. Savasana is the reward and the opportunity to reap all the benefits of the prior work.

Savasana is a time for transcendental meditation. A moment to free yourself from your thoughts and allow your mind to wander wherever it goes. The challenge here is to let go. There is no need to pull thoughts back in. If you have had a challenging physical, mental and emotional practice, your mind and body will welcome this time to just BE.

As you guide students out of Savasana, remember to cue students to:

- Deepen their breath.
- Return to the present moment.
- Reawaken their body, bring life back to muscles.

All of this should be guided with a soothing voice and slower tone. Finally, cue students to slowly with little effort, rise to a seat in easy pose and end with namaste.

CHAPTER ELEVEN

SETTING THE MOOD

THERE ARE different aspects to the yoga classroom environment including temperature, humidity, music, and lighting. However, since not everyone teaches in a hot studio, for simplicity sake, I will discuss music and lighting.

Music to Your Ears

I had never really thought about the need to download my playlist from Spotify. After all, the studio where I worked had wifi. What I didn't realize was that two devices could not play music at the same time and I had a basic Spotify plan, which I shared with my husband and kids. I was in the middle of my Yoga Sculpt Class and we were doing our cardio portion. I prepared a fast passed song to motivate my class for the full three minutes of cardio that included jumping jacks, burpees and running in place. In the middle of our cardio portion, my music spontaneously switched from "Who Let the Dogs Out" by Baha Men to a Randy Travis country song. I was completely shaken by this and at a loss of what to do to keep the class going. Each time I changed my music back, it would switch back to Randy Travis. I ended up shutting my music off altogether, and finished class without any music.

I was completely thrown, but I was able to continue on... because I had to. And you can too! We all mess up and have things happen that are out of our control. Trust that you can and will handle it. Needless to say, now I always download my music to avoid any potential issue with wifi cutting out.

If you use music from your phone for your class, besides downloading your playlists, I also suggest always switching your phone to Airplane Mode or Do Not Disturb. I had to learn this the hard way when my class was interrupted by a Skype call!

LET THERE BE LIGHT

Lighting can be a powerful tool in structuring your yoga class. Bright lights typically bring energy to students while dim lights will ground the student and relax them.

For this reason, I suggest using your lights as a tool to help your class have a satisfying arc from start (your intention) to close (savasana).

I start with my lights at an in-between level when I greet my students. This way, they can see me and yet still find a sense of calm before we start our flow in case anyone is new and perhaps nervous about launching into a yoga practice.

Then, when we are in our first posture, maybe child's pose, I turn the lights down more so that students can reflect and find their breath.

As we get into our flow, the lights become a bit brighter until they are at full brightness in the middle of class, or at my core workout section, when people need the most energy to continue.

After that, the lights will start their downward arc until they dim or maybe even are completely off during savanna. The effects of using lights in conjunction to music and your own voice with its rises and falls creates a powerful class environment.

You may be teaching in an environment where lights and music are not available to you or within your control. Keep the environment always in your mind when planning your class. Take note of where the sun is shining and have your students set up mats away from direct sunlight. Get creative with your environment. Consider passing out eye pillows for savasana.

CHAPTER TWELVE

EVERYONE STUMBLES

EVERY TEACHER MAKES MISTAKES. Even the most experienced teacher can have a momentary mental block — that time when they forget what comes next. The important thing to remember is that it happens. And when it happens, it's more important that you don't let this bother you. Easier said than done, but it's what will keep your students believing in your abilities.

It's one thing to make a mistake and laugh it off and move on. It's quite another to let it affect you and ruin your class. If you consider your students first, then you will remember that you want them to feel comfortable rather than bad for you. So if you stumble, simply make it part of the dance.

CLASS CHALLENGES

We've discussed sequencing at length because it is the first thing that teachers consider when preparing their class. However, there are other elements of a strong class that can also be challenging for new teachers. Below are some of the challenges that new teachers face when structuring a class:

- Managing time
- Mastering environment
- Keeping students engaged

Figuring out how to time your yoga class can be the first hurdle a new yoga teacher faces. When I think back to the first few yoga classes I taught in the studio, I remember three big fears:

1. Too much time. I feared that I would finish my sequence too early and not have something to do to fill up the hour.
2. Going over time. Not having enough time for cool down and savasana or God forbid, I ran the class over an hour.
3. I did not time my music right and my music would end too early and I didn't have an appropriate song for the close of class.

Time management and understanding the time allotment for each part of your yoga sequence is an important part of teaching, and it is also something that comes naturally with experience.

When you break out your groups of postures, you will know how much time to devote to each section and you can follow your playlist accordingly. For instance, you may find that your spine strengthening series comes in around 5 minutes to complete 3 postures with 3-5 cues for each. You can have a playlist and plan to find a 5–6-minute song for that section. I suggest going over a little bit longer than 5 minutes, so you build in some time and not freak out when your next song comes on. You can always skip to the next song if you finish your section early.

Another way to address music is to find extended songs that play for 15 minutes or so and have a similar beat with no words so that you do not have to mess with the music at all. It basically serves as a backdrop and does not take prominence in the class.

There are several playlists you can find on Spotify or Pandora that are specifically designed for whatever type of yoga class you teach.

TIME MANAGEMENT TIPS AND TRICKS

Tip 1: Use music to cue time.

Tip 2: Hold students in postures for longer periods of time. This may be intentional, but it is also a great back pocket trick. You can deepen your students with cuing or allow for some silence. Don't be afraid to hold your students in a posture. They can explore this way.

Tip 3: Return to Sun A when needed. Students are familiar with repetition with Sun A and it is a great fall back.

Tip 4: Add a filler pose when needed. There are several tricks to "fill in gaps" between your blocks, between different sides and when you "forget" what comes next or find you have extra time. Some of my go to postures are:

- Prayer Twist
- Hold in Plank
- Reverse Plank
- Child's Pose

Tip 5: Do not worry about talking too much during a sequence. Focus on directional cues, encouragement cues and modifications for safety and up-level options. With time, you will pepper in additional cues such as the benefits of the posture and some interesting random facts. Make sure you only speak to what you know.

Tip 6: Challenge your students. Balancing is one way to add intensity and focus. Long holds are another.

Tip 7: Limit the use of words that imply there is a goal for mastering a posture. Every posture will look different in different bodies. Students should be encouraged to listen to their body and take what they need. I like to steer away from statements like "find your edge" unless I know my student base.

Not every student is doing yoga to challenge their capabilities. The more you teach, the more you will get a feel for what your students need. When you have an established rapport, you will have more license to speak direct to your students and you can push them, if that is indeed what they are seeking. If in doubt, keep it general.

KEEPING STUDENTS ENGAGED

Keeping students engaged throughout class can be a source of nervousness for many teachers. Your sequence, intention, and the way you cue your students will ensure that they are mentally as well as physically engaged.

There are many sources to find inspiration for class including sequence building software, YouTube videos, flash cards, books, and other yoga classes.

Because there are so many options available, this is another reason your binder will come in handy. Once you figure out a method for building sequences that work for you, you can keep track of all the fun sequences that you have built in one place that is easy to access.

There are several different online yoga sequence builders that you can draw inspiration from. Tummee, as mentioned before, is one of my favorite sequence builders because it has an extensive collection of postures as well as variations of postures. Tummee uses a simple drag and drop system that allows you to build a sequence in minutes. With so many options, you will likely find ideas and sources of inspiration to keep your sequences fresh and new. You'll also discover new ways to warm up the body and restore it after the challenging portion of the sequence.

In many yoga sequence builders, you can create your own classes and then save them for a later date. This can save you time.

You'll also have access to sequences created by other teachers. Observing how other teachers piece poses together or work towards a peak pose can give you ideas in your own classes.

For those of you who are tactile learners, you might find yoga flash cards helpful. With flash cards, you can easily fan out or lay your cards on the floor like a storybook and make easy changes to the order. This can help you to see a sequence in its entirety and see if it works.

Be mindful that not all sequences that are published and available are safe or practical. With so many options to choose from, you can also easily become overwhelmed. Make sure to practice your sequence in your own body. This really is the only way to know if your sequence makes sense.

STUDENT ENGAGEMENT TIPS & TRICKS

Some of the best ways to spur inspiration include taking a variety of styles of yoga classes. Take notes after classes to keep ideas fresh in your mind and immediately file your notes in your binder.

If you enjoy a particular sequence, ask the teacher if they will share it with you. More than likely the teacher will be flattered and happy to share. Remember that even if you teach the same sequence, it will always be a different class.

Supplement your studies and practice with anatomy or body work classes and strength building, Pilates, Barre or other fitness classes. Sometimes you will learn more about why a posture or sequence works or does not work when you understand body mechanics. You also can throw in tidbits of body knowledge throughout your class, which will only add credibility to your teaching.

If you are unsure of how your sequence is being received, ask students to give you feedback. Another option is to teach a class on Zoom and record it so you can play it back for review.

. . .

THE COMPARISON GAME

External challenges are normal. Practice and time in the studio will help you meet the challenges of time management, music and lighting, and keeping students engaged. But there is another challenge that you might face. This one is internal... the comparison game.

Many yoga teachers are paid for classes based on the number of students who attend. Because of this, it can be hard to not let yourself get caught up in the numbers. If you only have a few students signed up for your class, and the class after yours is filled to capacity, it's hard to not let your ego takeover.

Thoughts of: "I must not be a very good teacher" or "they like that teacher better than me," are bound to float into your head.

As Covid-19 restrictions began to ease and we returned to teaching, but were holding classes outside, my numbers were the lowest out of all the teachers from the studio. This kept me up at night. Here I was a seasoned teacher approaching two years and new teachers were filling their classes. I started to wonder "Am I too old?" "Do people not like me?" and other doubting thoughts.

I had filled the room during my regularly timed schedule. I had regulars who gave me positive feedback, telling me how much they loved my class and bringing me little gifts here and there. I had a rapport with my students. They knew me and we had a chemistry. With the new class times, I always seemed to be teaching to new faces. But they were not returning to my classes. I started to get hung up on this fact and question my own abilities. I wondered whether I was the only one with this issue.

I considered quitting several times because I didn't feel that my self esteem was worth losing sleep over. But I persevered and taught my classes the way that I do and some classes would end and I would be validated and other times I would be left wondering what happened. But all in all, I never gave up and just kept teaching and trying not to let the way it must have looked to other teachers and my managers get the best of me. I had to pull up my big girl pants and remind myself of all the yoga concepts that I learned and this was also the impetus I needed to write this book. I was reminded of what it was like to teach for the first time. I overcame my confidence problem, but here it was rearing its little head again. But since writing this book, I have pushed through my ego and you know what? My classes are getting bigger.

Part of the reason behind smaller classes has nothing to do with the teacher. I was teaching during Covid. There could be a million reasons why students did not come to class. What this period helped me accomplish was to refine my teaching style, my niche, and what is unique about what I offer.

I am reminded that old habits die hard. When those negative thoughts began to creep back into my awareness, I had to stop it in its tracks, slay my ego, and come back to all the progress and growth I have made. Acknowledge the thoughts and then get back in my own lane and remember this is my journey and mine alone.

Another thing to remember is that not being a good teacher is just one of the infinite possibilities of why someone is not taking your class. Ask yourself what other reasons could there be? There are many possible reasons that students are not attending your class, many of which have nothing to do with your talent as a yoga teacher or your likability.

If you're new to teaching or you're feeling low because of a small class turnout, consider these factors:

TIME SLOTS

Depending on where you live, there are certain yoga time slots that are deemed the "prime time." Prime time is before and after work from 6-8 a.m. and 5-7 p.m. These classes are easy for people who work full-time to attend before or after work and still make it home in time to cook dinner.

These classes will often see higher attendance than classes closer to midday or in the early morning hours. Mid morning from 8-11 a.m. and late afternoon from 2-5 p.m. may draw a good crowd of stay-at-home parents or those who work from home. Daytime weekend classes often have good attendance rates, but the consistency of students can be less predictable as people's weekend plans vary.

LOCATION

Location is key because distance and ease of travel can impact attendance. Public transportation access, parking and traffic times all become considerations to factor in. Studios can have an advantage with a business crowd if location is walking distance to many businesses. Conversely, studios in residential areas can attract those traveling from home.

LOCAL COMPETITION

The number of yoga practitioners in relation to the number of yoga studios in the area will impact class attendance. If you're in an area with many other yoga studios, then the amount of students in the area are dispersed over many different studios.

WEATHER CONDITIONS

Instead of competing with other yoga studios, the weather brings about competition to other activities. Nice weather may entice students to be in nature. Cold weather can make it challenging to get to class for both road conditions and motivation.

NEW TEACHER BIAS

I have met several students who have said to me that when they see a new name on the schedule, they choose to not come to class. People are creatures of habit and like I mentioned, want to know what to expect. Unfortunately, the mere fact of being new is a deterrent for many.

We're Human, After All

Try not to compare yourself with other teachers or look to student numbers as a barometer of whether or not you are a good teacher. Similarly, don't kick yourself if you make a mistake.

Look, we all mess up. We do it because we are human. 90% of the time, students do not even notice. And 99% of the time, students do not care. What matters is how you react.

- Do not draw attention to it.
- Do not let it make you lose confidence.
- Quickly move on.
- Incorporate any mistake into your sequence.
- Have a sense of humor.

Banish Nerves

The inclination of new teachers is to admit that you know you messed up, but trust me, you only draw more attention to a mistake and can lose the respect of your students. Students want to feel like they are in safe hands. Confidence is key. Replace "I'm sorry" with "rather"....

If a mistake is totally obvious, maybe say, "Hey guys, I'm human. I forgot the left side. Let's make up for it now so you are not walking funny when you leave here."

When you do get nervous, look at your students and find an anchor. Focus on someone who is smiling back in agreement when you introduce yourself or someone who knows the sequence or has been practicing a long time in the event you forget anything.

Always look at bodies if you cannot seem to find the cues you are looking for. It's okay to hold your students in a posture. It is actually better to give them some time to process. Silence can serve as space for students to process and for you to "remember" where you left off.

You can always breathe with your students while you collect yourself.

Put Yourself in the Seat of your Student

Imagine or visualize when you are a student. Are you judging the teacher? Do you care if he or she makes a mistake? My guess is NO... unless he or she does not roll with it or fix it.

How much attention are you paying to the music? Chances are you are focused in trying to understand and hear the cues, process what was said, and get your body into the pose.

The things your students *will* notice are weird transitions, feeling unbalanced in their bodies or if you miss an entire side. Your students may notice they do not have time to breathe or the teacher is moving too quickly or not quick enough. Think of those things as you move through your class. Learn to read your students' body language.

Are the majority of your students in child's pose during a balancing posture? This could indicate that your sequence is too challenging or that you have put too much focus on one leg. If this is a heated class, maybe you have your temperature set too high.

Are the majority of your students jumping ahead in a breath to movement flow? This could indicate you are moving too slowly, cuing or talking too much and not cuing to move breath to movement.

Your student is not going to remember your playlist or be "sick" of it. Repetition with minor tweaks is the aim. By simply changing the music, tone, and intention, you can make a completely different class with the same sequence. Maybe you switch the order of your mini block flows or an easy change is to add a different arm variation. When you have a simple framework in which to build your class, you will be able to focus on your students and less on "remembering your lines".

You are not there to impress and perform. Your role is to create a safe and inviting experience for students to explore. I'll discuss safety more in the next chapter.

CHAPTER THIRTEEN

SAFETY FIRST

YOUR ABILITY TO cue and communicate proper alignment as well as your understanding of basic anatomy and biomechanics, not only makes you sound credible as a teacher, it also helps to keep your students safe.

Biomechanics is the study of movement of a living body, including how muscles, bones, tendons, and ligaments work together to move. There are countless books out there that can give you a working knowledge of body movement in yoga.

Often, instead of doing research, teachers will repeat cues they have heard from other teachers... cues that not only do not make sense, but are clearly unsafe.

When I polled yoga teachers regarding what they wished they had received more training in. Surprisingly, anatomy was not high on the list. Anatomy came in at 46%. Sequence building was number 1 and philosophy and history was number 2. Yet, if a student were to injure themselves in your class, I guarantee that you would feel devastated. Safety comes from a strong knowledge of anatomy and alignment. Keeping your students safe is paramount to being a yoga teacher.

Now that I am approaching 50 and I am starting to feel my

body change, safety and alignment has become more of a priority for me. Students comes in all sizes and ages. Students should expect you are well trained and will keep them safe in your care.

Remember that you are not a physical therapist or a medical doctor. You are not responsible for the health of your students. However, students trust you to keep them safe. Always ask before you offer adjustments. I recommend sticking with non-evasive, simple adjustments such as relaxing the shoulders down the back or extending a student's arms out in a warrior 2. In savasana, a gentle massage on the back of the neck or cradling the ankles can aid in a state of relaxation. Avoid touching a student's joints unless you are doing a private and have intimate knowledge of their health condition and have experience with the particular adjustment you are doing. Not all bodies are the same and you can do some serious damage if you do not know what you are doing. When in doubt, it is always safer to avoid hands-on adjustments.

A good yoga instructor will have a class designed incorporating strength, balance, and flexibility. A thoughtful class will have an adequate warm-up period allowing the body to open and muscles to warm. A safe class will balance the body by working both front and back planes of the body as well as equally working left and right sides. In her book, *The Sequencing Bible*, Eleanor Evrard offers some advice to keep in mind regarding safety:

- Try to avoid adding more than 3 standing postures balancing on one leg in any given sequence. More than this may be difficult for beginners and seniors.
- Be cautious of moving from opening and closing hip rotation.

I would add:

- Take a look at a student's foot placement and avoid torquing the knee by switching foot placement back and forth.
- Offer generous opportunities to modify and level up.

Remind students that yoga is an individual practice. Not all bodies are identical. Encourage students to acknowledge how postures feel in their own bodies. This can be reinforced several times during class to help them tune in to their body sensations.

I always tell students that if something hurts, don't do it. Yoga should never hurt.

Following are safety tips and facts specific to each body part that are helpful to keep in mind when sequencing.

The Foot

The foot has a total of 26 bones and 32 joints. When we stand, 100% of our body weight passes through our feet.

Problems with your knee can be affected by problems with your feet.

Transitions that include bending the knee between postures can be helpful to students with SI, lower back and knee problems.

In standing poses, the first foundation is our feet. Where we position our feet will impact where and how we position our hips. This is most notable in postures such as triangle or revolved triangle and pyramid pose.

The Knee

Unless there is direct stress or injury to the knee, pain in the knee may be due to overuse of the hip or ankle joint. Because of this, it is recommended to include hip and ankle range rotations during warm-up.

When the knee makes direct contact on the mat (camel, table top, heroes pose), we can add additional pressure to the knee so it is helpful to cushion the knees even if they are not in pain because over time with repetitive use, we can cause degeneration and arthritic changes to the knee joint.

The quadriceps are powerful stabilizers of the knee joint and we can feel them work in warrior and crescent poses.

Tight hamstrings also impact the knee.

Engaging the glutes and the hamstrings in warrior 1 will prevent the hips from sinking toward the floor and help protect undo pressure on the knee.

Always cue to micro-bend your knee when balancing. Even in postures such as warrior 3, dancer's and half moon, you should cue to micro-bend your standing knee. When you bend your standing knee, you engage your stabilizing muscles, which help build more strength.

THE PELVIS

Your pelvis is what attaches the top and lower parts of your body. It is central to how we move and stabilize the force of gravity.

Yoga can help you practice and train your body to get up and down from the floor, which is good for aging. In terms of aging, the pelvic floor is an important muscle to maintain.

Women may be familiar with Kegel exercises, which are often suggested during pregnancy. However, reality is that these exercises are important throughout life in order to maintain health and avoid incontinence with age.

THE PSOAS

The psoas is the single most important postural and structural muscle in the body. The psoas muscle is located in the lower lumbar region of the spine and connects to the leg bone. Because of this location, the psoas muscle is always associated with the core of our body.

Its function is related to posture, balance and breath. Without the psoas, everyday movement such as walking would not be possible since it is the only muscle that connects your spine to your legs. In addition to flexing the hip, this core muscle works to stabilize the spine and regulate breathing.

Your psoas and SI joint (sacroiliac joint) are intricately linked. The sacroiliac joint links your pelvis and lower spine. When the SI joint is overstretched, it will shorten and weaken the psoas muscles.

Postures that help stretch and strengthen the psoas are warrior 1, pigeon pose, and lunges.

THE HIPS

Our torso rests on top of our hips. Our hips are what keep us balanced and level.

Keeping a micro-bend in your knee in poses that allow for extreme depth beyond normal range of motion will help you avoid hyperextension.

Hip rotations during warm up will help with hip mobility and can help avoid lower back pain.

THE LOWER BACK

Our bodies are interconnected. Issues with one area can affect another. For instance, lack of mobility due to tightness in the hips is a common cause of knee and lower back pain.

To support, improve, and even build strength in the back, spine strengthening and stretching poses are recommended. These include cobra and sphinx pose to help the middle and upper back region. Bridge pose is also good for strengthening the spine and relieving lower back pain.

According to the World Health Organization, lower back pain accounts for the highest amount of days missed from work worldwide. Yoga is one of the most recommended forms of treatment for lower back pain. (Wynne-Jones et al., 2013)

Lying on your back with your legs up a wall is a great neutralizer for your lower back. Supported bridge, rag doll and wide leg forward fold also help to decompress the spine.

With a mind on lower back safety, always cue students to bend their knees in a standing or wide legged forward fold.

The Glutes

Most often, the glute muscles get overly tight when you spend a lot of time sitting, especially with crossed legs or crossed ankles.

The glutes are part of the posterior chain. The posterior chain is the group of muscles that run down the entire backside of your body. The posterior chain is what propels us forward.

One of the muscles located in the glute region is the piriformis muscle. If one piriformis muscle is tighter than the other it can negatively affect the balance of the sacroiliac joint, causing pain and/or instability. Weakness in this area will limit your ability to balance on one leg.

The piriformis muscle is close to the sciatic nerve. When it is tight it can cause nerve pain that starts at the glutes and travels down the back of the leg and into the foot.

Postures that help stretch a tight piriformis muscle can be practiced in prone positions, seated, or standing. They include half pigeon, figure four, supine figure four, butterfly pose, deer pose, seated straddle, supine twist, dragon pose, and others.

THE SHOULDERS

Our shoulders allow us to reach. Most shoulder and wrist injuries are caused by everyday movements.

The two most common movements we do in yoga that place excessive strain on our shoulders are vinyasa flows that include chaturangas and reaching our arms overhead. Note that my use of the word "chaturanga" implies the flow that includes the four postures: high plank, low plank (chaturanga), upward facing dog and downward facing dog.

Alternatives to chaturangas to protect your shoulders and wrists as well as strain from repetitive movement include avoiding the push up portion and replacing plank with tabletop. From here, you can add a cow or cobra in place of upward facing dog and simply push back to downward facing dog. Or, include a child's pose before pushing back to downward facing dog.

When bringing your arms overhead in mountain pose, try to send your arms upwards using shoulder flexion instead of abduction. In other words, instead of "circle sweep" your arms (sending arms away from your side body), send your arms up in a forward motion toward the top of your mat with your thumbs leading up.

THE ELBOWS

Elbows like knees, should always be in a micro-bend. Otherwise, hyperextension can produce bone on bone compression.

By keeping a micro-bend in the elbow, you also help prevent your wrists from too much strain.

THE WRISTS AND HANDS

How we place our hands will affect how much pressure is placed on our wrists.

Keep your wrist parallel to the front of your mat. Avoid dumping your body weight in the heel of your hand. You want to position your hand as though you are going to pick up the mat by a hand grip (think of palming a basketball). You want to imagine sticky fingertips. Create some space at the center of your inner palm. Like with your feet, equally distribute the weight in the four corners of your palm.

HEAD AND NECK

Our head and neck can feel stress when we put too much pressure on our cervical spine.

Instead of looking up or tilting your head back in a backbend like cobra pose, keep your head in a neutral position by imagining a string pulling the crown of your head toward the top of your mat, lifting your chest (not your head) off your mat.

Some of the most serious yoga injuries are due to headstands. As a new yoga instructor, I would avoid cuing for shoulder stand, handstands, headstands, and tripod headstands altogether. Advanced yogis can up level at their own risk.

WHEN WE PLACE OUR BODIES IN INTENTIONAL WAYS, WE MUST be mindful of our anatomy. There are always modifications that you can offer as a teacher. Remind your students that they are their best guide and if they have an existing injury, some postures may need to be avoided altogether.

It is possible to overstretch, especially in a heated yoga class. Lengthening your ligaments or tendons too far can put undo stress on them.

If you ever feel sharp or shooting sensations or numbness, immediately adjust your position to relieve the pain. Yoga should never hurt.

Most common injuries experienced during yoga are due to the following:

- Muscles not being adequately warmed up.
- Overuse and repetition without a counter posture for balance.
- Improper placement of hands and feet.
- Rotating from one plane to another without safe transitions.
- Overextending twists. Not easing into a posture.
- Locking joints by hyper-extending past your normal range of motion.
- Weak supporting muscles.

Before teaching a new sequence, make sure you have practiced the sequence in your body. Notice how it feels in your body and make sure you do not have any awkward transitions.

CHAPTER FOURTEEN

WHAT DID YOU SAY?

THE WAY you cue students in and out of poses is an important aspect of your teaching and imperative to your success as a teacher.

When students cannot hear you or readily follow your cues, the result will be frustration, looking around the room at other students, and overall confusion. On the other hand, if your cues are clear, students will be engaged and will move as you intended.

The most important thing when cuing is to be heard and understood. Simplify your cues especially when you are just beginning to teach. It is most important to communicate effectively so that your student can safely get into a posture. Stick with the basic cue formula: breath, verb, body part, direction. All other cues will be peppered in as your confidence grows.

Methods to simplify your cues include:

- Avoid scientific, anatomical terms and Sanskrit.
- Use visual anchors in the room such as, "Cactus your arms to the green wall."
- Look to student's bodies for cues. "Press through your front leg," or "Anchor your back heel down."

- Instead of saying the words left and right, you can say "second side" or "switch legs."

You might want to type out your entire script with every cue. This is a great exercise to get used to how to cue. You will probably not look at the script ever again, but just typing it out word-for-word will help secure it into your subconscious.

If you can, video record yourself teaching the class or record your voice teaching a class. It is helpful to say the words out loud and not just whisper them in your head.

CONSIDER THE FOLLOWING CUING SUGGESTIONS:

Cue from the Ground Up

With the exception of your first cue that gets people into the pose, such as mountain pose when you might say, "Lift your arms to the sky," it's a good practice to cue from the ground up. This method ensures that students are balanced and safe.

Below is an example of cuing from the ground up for mountain pose:

- Press down through both feet
- Square your hips to the front of your space
- Pull your belly into your spine
- Soften your shoulders away from your ears
- Extend the crown of your head to the sky

Feet and Hand Placement Cues

- Find a heel to arch alignment
- Pivot your feet toward the long side of your mat
- Face your palms up
- Spread your fingers wide

GAZE/VISUAL CUES

- Look toward the top of your mat
- Rest your eyes on an unmoving spot for balance (your *drishti*)
- Gaze at your navel
- Imagine a string lifting you up from the crown of your head.
- Energetically split the mat apart with your feet.

Modifications and Up Level Cues

Make sure to word modifications and up leveling as options or suggestions. You may want to reiterate that every day and every practice is different and remind students to draw attention to where they are today in their posture.

For example in a revolved crescent, you can cue:

- Option to gaze over your shoulder to challenge your balance
- Or option to gaze down for grounding

Encouragement Cues

As a new teacher, keeping your cues simple should be your primary focus. Adding in encouragement and health benefit cues will organically make their way into your class with time.

Adding student names is always great for rapport and encouragement. However, be mindful of calling someone out for specific capabilities and instead, focus on keeping encouragement general. We want to avoid drawing comparisons in class. Suggestions for encouragement cues include:

- Good, Kelly
- Nice focus, Jean

- Stay with me
- Make this your strongest set
- Power through
- Almost there
- Yes you can
- No judgements
- Feel the comfort of gravity's pull
- Because you can
- With change you get change
- Tap into your strength
- Nice adjustment
- Love your energy
- Way to bring it today
- You've got this

Focus Cues

- Tune into the present.
- Notice where you might be feeling tightness. How can you ease up, but still embrace the pose?
- Pay attention to what you are feeling in your body right now.
- Take note of what emotions are coming up for you.
- Draw your intention inward.
- Ask yourself what thoughts have crept into your mind. Can you acknowledge the thoughts and let them go without judgment?
- Breathe
- Where do you feel this?
- Come back to center.

Anatomy Cues
These cues work for most postures:

- Stack your joints.
- Press through the four corners of your feet.
- Spread your fingers/toes wide.
- Engage your core.
- Maintain length in the back of your neck.

Safety Cues

Focus on what you want students to do, rather than what you do not want students to do. For example, in an extended warrior pose, try to stay away from this type of cue, even though it may be accurate: "Avoid dumping weight into your front quad." Instead, suggest this: " Lift up through your obliques to take pressure off your front knee.

For joint safety, emphasize strength and stability rather than promoting more flexibility.

For supine postures, suggest students keep their back flat to the mat and pull their belly into their spine.

For prone postures, recommend students to press the mat away and dome out their upper spine. Or, lengthen through the crown of your head to protect your cervical spine.

FOLLOWING ARE MORE CUES THAT WILL HELP STUDENTS protect their joints:

Wrists

- Spread your fingers wide.
- Press evenly into your index finger and thumb.
- Roll out your wrists.

Elbows

- Maintain no more than a 90 degree bend in your arms.
- Hug your elbows by your sides.

BEYOND YOGA TEACHER TRAINING: 101

- Micro bend your elbows.

Knees

- Keep your knee stacked over your ankle.
- Micro bend your knees.

Hips

- Utilizing blocks can help to avoid over stretching your hips.
- Only move as deep as is comfortable.

Shoulders

- Relax your shoulders away from your ears.
- Squeeze your should blades together and down your back.

Head and Neck

- Keep your neck long.
- Lengthen through the crown of your head.
- Pull your shoulders down your back.

Lower Back

- Pull your belly into your spine.
- Micro bend your knees.
- Lengthen your tailbone toward your mat.

Below is a list of action words that can help keep your cues fresh and new.

Lengthen	Embrace	Ground	Tip	Twist
Open	Cuddle	Plant	Tilt	Spiral
Expand	Squeeze	Glue	Tuck	Wind
Stretch	Curl	Secure	Scoop	Rotate
Reach	Coil	Fasten	Knit	Wring
Elongate	Nestle	Pin	Shift	Spin
Shine	Draw	Zip	Roll	Swivel
Rise	Guide	Latch	Point	Shift
Sweep	Send	Join	Float	Position
Spread	Direct	Connect	Hug	Roll
Widen	Place	Seal	Arc	Angle
Straighten	Cup	Stabilize	Hollow	Transfer
Broaden	Cradle	Tack	Arch	Rinse
Peel	Grab	Adhere	Dome	Anchor
Fan	Press	Root	Flex	Merge

Level	Rest	Tighten	Adjust	Activate
Align	Relax	Grasp	Refine	Turn On
Track	Soften	Hinge	Zero In	Engage
Parallel	Release	Grip	Locate	Simulate
Square	Melt	Clutch	Focus	Ignite
Balance	Drop	Grab	Aim	Trigger
Equalize	Hang	Squeeze	Targe	Fuel
Flush	Drape	Shorten	Arrange	Fire Up
Stack	Dangle	Compress	Glide	Cultivate
Regulate	Sink	Contract	Shimmy	Rainbow
Hold	Surrender	Hold	Cross	Velcro
Maintain	Disengage	Resist	Wrap	Lock
Endure	Turn Off	Attach	Hook	Bind
Sit With	Observe	Affix	Interlace	Round

FEEL FREE TO USE AND BORROW THIS EXTENSIVE LIST OF CUES, but also have the confidence to find your own. The result will be a class that is uniquely you.

CHAPTER FIFTEEN

STRUT YOUR STUFF

WHAT IS the most important characteristic of a yoga teacher? You would be surprised to learn that it is not how flexible you are or how beautiful you make the shapes. Most important is a teacher who can lead and lead multiple skill levels. So, if you ever had a job working in a fast-paced restaurant and had to think on your feet, know that your skills mastered will be far more valuable than doing a side crow.

A good yoga teacher:

- Knows who he/she is.
- Knows what they know and what they do not know.
- Knows how to connect with students.
- Does one thing well and cuts themselves slack on everything else.

I know my energy, enthusiasm, and ability to laugh at myself is my strength. I also know not everyone appreciates my sense of humor. I am able to laugh at myself and that puts people at ease. I know that I am not always on beat for my Sculpt class so I will throw out a joke about that sometimes.

One thing I did that some may find cheesy, but I found it to be extremely effective in engaging my students was to ask, "What time is it?" before we did hammer curls. They came to expect this and looked forward to it and they responded in a rousing, "Hammer time!" It was silly, but it was unique to my class.

Sometimes a class may have a great technical instructor, but the teacher is boring or aloof. Other times a class can be fun, but the instructor lacks experience.

As a teacher, you create an experience for your students. When your students are able to be fully engaged in the present moment, that is what turns a good class to an exceptional one. That is the transformational class. It won't happen all the time, even to the best of teachers.

What qualities elevate a good teacher to a great teacher whose class stands out?

Ability to Connect

Using names, eye contact and a smile goes a long way to connect with your students to help them feel comfortable and a sense of belonging.

Command of the Class

A successful teacher must have the attention of their students. When a teacher can walk around the room and appropriately read the room and adjust the class accordingly, they have a command of the class. A confident teacher gains trust from their students and can sustain their attention.

Energy Level

It can be challenging for students to hold a posture. Depending on the class, this can vary, but you do want to challenge your students. Unless it is your intention, it is better to challenge your students, not put them to sleep.

Personality

Although people are drawn to teachers for a variety of reasons, showcasing your unique personality allows you to better connect with your ideal student.

Preparation

Great yoga teachers are prepared to teach. They may leave room for spontaneity in class, but they are there on time and have their music, lighting, and room ready for their students upon arrival.

Flexibility

Flexibility is important not just for your body. Great certified yoga instructors adjust their teaching based on their audience. They have a plan, but that plan can be changed on the fly to cater to their audience. There is a certain intuition required, to listen and care for your students, even if they are not directly giving you feedback.

Passion

When a teacher loves teaching and loves yoga, it shows. Passion is infectious. A great teacher has a desire to inspire.

Knowledge

A great yoga teacher knows about yoga and can easily cue poses and benefits, knows where the student feels something in their body, and can speak to what the student is likely experiencing. This builds trust. It comes with practice and self study.

Safety

A great yoga teacher will watch their students, making sure no one is going to get injured and cues for safety and alignment.

———

HOWEVER, ONE CAN DO ALL OF THESE THINGS AND STILL FIND that students come and go. There are a multitude of reasons why students may not be in your class such as their schedule changing, their responsibilities changing, or maybe their passion for the discipline changing.

However, if you are doing something in class that has an adverse reaction with students, that's another story. Ashley Hagen, Yoga Teacher and Coach (www.ashleyrosehagen.com)

covers the top 4 reasons she found that students do not return to class:

Unwanted Adjustments

Always ask. While students' eyes are closed, say something like... I like to offer hands on assists and adjustments in class to help with deepening, alignment, and safety. If for any reason you would prefer not to be touched today, please raise a hand while everyone's eyes are closed, and I will make sure to honor your request and respect your space.

Ego and Self-promotion

Always serve your students first. There is no room for ego as a yoga teacher. You also are a student of yoga, and you are leading your class through your actions. If you have information to provide to help the student such as when you teach next, that is great, but do not use the forum to self-promote.

Gossip and Non-inclusiveness

Your job as a yoga instructor is to provide a safe space where students feel comfortable to explore their practice. Yoga is about union, belonging, and connectedness. Gossip on or off the mat or bad-mouthing others especially other teachers, studios, and students will make you lose your credibility and respect. Think kindness, friendliness, and create an inviting environment.

Preaching an Agenda or Belief

Never use your platform to push your own agenda or beliefs. Unless your class is promoted with a specialized population, you should leave any political, spiritual, or religious positions at the door. This includes lifestyle, nutrition, and alternative medicine. Even though yoga comes from India and is rooted in Hindu philosophy, please always keep your intentions general, universal, and abstract enough so that that student can interpret it to fit their circumstance.

I agree fully with Hagan's suggestions and I'd like to add one more...

NEVER Burn Bridges

If you work for a studio, do not bad talk your co-workers, managers, owners, or students. Besides being un-yoga like, it can result in a lawsuit and damage your reputation.

OTHER COMMON MISTAKES MADE BY NEW YOGA TEACHERS include:

- Assuming alignment is one size fits all.

It's important to realize that all bodies are different and that just because a pose does not look like it is "supposed" to doesn't mean a student should be adjusted.

- Thinking you must have an answer.

Students will look to you for all kinds of guidance. You may get asked physical therapy questions, health questions, etc. It is always best to let a student know that they should ask a doctor for medical advice and if there is something you do not know, you can always say I am not sure, but let me do a little research and get back to you. This is a great opportunity to make a connection with a student.

- New teachers do not need to say yes to every class offered.

Burn out is a real thing and over-extending yourself will only have a negative effect on you and your teaching. I found it better to start with 1 or 2 permanent classes, but be open to subbing for others or looking at other alternative teaching situations.

- You do not need to always have an inspirational message and transforming class. It is not realistic.

There is no need to prepare an elaborate class with complicated transitions.

You've Got This!

- Never apologize for messing up or forgetting something.
- After a slow flow and before a fast flow, it can be helpful to say "listen for changes". This not only reminds students to listen to cues and be present, but also gives you a little leeway if you miss a step.
- Teach in as many environments as you can. This will only strengthen your ability to adjust.
- Fake it until you make it. We all suffer from imposter syndrome from time to time. Practice is the only thing that will help you improve your teaching and make you more confident.
- Remember that the students are having a different experience than you are as a teacher. They are not there to watch you. They are there for their own practice. You are there to serve them.

Develop Good Habits

- Introduce yourself.

- Makes eye contact with students and acknowledge them by using names throughout the class.

- Always offer modifications.

- Great teachers check in with their students and read their body cues.

- Make sure all students feel welcome and included.

- Face toward your students, not away.

- Find moments of silence.

- Demo postures that may be complicated or difficult to explain.

- Keep your sequence simple. You can add more challenging postures and more creative transitions after you have built your confidence.

- Manage light, sound, and other ambiance so the environment feels comfortable and serene.

- Have a plan, but maintain flexibility to meet students at their level.

- Maintain a personal practice.

- Be approachable. A great teacher is open to questions. However, a wise teacher will encourage a student to find their own answers within.

- Adjust with confidence. If you are hesitant, forget hands-on adjusting altogether.

- Continue your yoga studies and find a specialty.

A 200-hour teacher training is only the beginning of the journey. Think of it as your general education. Self-study and continued education are paramount. This may include workshops, additional trainings, conferences, reading, and personal study.

Common New Teacher Habits to Avoid

- Do not call someone out by name for doing their own thing.
- Do not look at your phone.
- Do not talk too much. Give your students a little silence to process and tune in.
- Do not use yoga jargon without an explanation.
- If you do not know or remember the anatomical correct name of body parts or how to pronounce a Sanskrit word, do not attempt to say it.
- Do not pretend to be a doctor and give health or medical advice EVER!

New Teacher Pitfalls

Watch out for burnout. New teachers have a tendency to take on too much. Be careful of subbing too much. When you are too available to sub, others may take advantage of your availability and ask you to cover. It's best to offer trades so that your own yoga practice doesn't get forgotten. It's easy to fall into the trap of prioritizing teaching over practicing.

Most importantly, remember that a great yoga teacher is present, not "perfect."

CHAPTER SIXTEEN

YOUR YOGA BRAND

STUDENTS WILL GRAVITATE toward teachers they connect with. Your class should be a reflection of your personality. However, as you have probably experienced in life, it is impossible to please all the people all the time. For every person that thinks you talk too much before class, there will be another who says your message was exactly what they needed to hear. For every person who loves your playlist, there will be someone who complains about it.

Even though you can't please everyone all of the time, you certainly can please a well-defined group of people who are looking for something that you, and only you, can offer most of the time.

This is why you need to find the people who resonate with you and your class. Your fans will come back. Encourage students to try other teachers and stress that yoga is not one size fits all. This is a way to encourage and inspire students even when you are not the best fit for them.

We talked about what is unique about you and hopefully you have jotted down a few of your strengths and have a general idea about who your ideal student is. Now it is time to marry those two ideas to find your niche.

. . .

CREATE A NICHE

A yoga niche is what makes you and your class stand out from others. Mark Stephens describes this as "a teacher's palette of styles" in his book, *Teaching Yoga*. This is where your creativity comes into play. You get to design something that is uniquely yours. This specialty will be your brand and style. In short, it's your niche and like you, it will evolve over time. Because you are still new to teaching yoga, I would not branch out into too many different niches. But for brainstorming purposes, I would go to town and write down every different niche that you have any possible interest in. You can narrow it down from there. Once you build your following, you can always expand and grow, but for now, I suggest you focus on one niche at a time.

Pay attention to the teachers and classes that you are attracted to. What do you like about a specific class or approach to yoga? Do you like when a teacher talks about yoga philosophy, focuses on anatomy or chakras, or incorporates guided meditation in class?

Make a list of your favorite yoga teachers and write down a couple of aspects that make them who they are. What is their focus? Can you identify what their yoga niche is?

WHY A NICHE IS IMPORTANT

Marketing becomes much easier when you can target your ideal student. By narrowing your focus, you can become an expert in your specific niche, which will build credibility and your reputation as being the "go to person" for that particular niche. This allows you to more easily build your brand, reputation, and stand out from the crowd.

I have seen teachers pair yoga with hiking, yoga with rock climbing, yoga with kids, yoga with wine, and more. The combinations are endless. Yoga for people living with MS, trauma yoga, chess and yoga... you get the idea!

After you've found your niche, here are a few ways to put it to use.

- Theme classes around your niche such as, "Gentle yoga for back injuries."
- Use your niche as a roadway to become an "expert" in your area. Do this by continually learning about the topic, connect with others in a similar field, perhaps even do speaking engagements paired with your yoga niche. In time, you will be perceived as an expert in your area.
- Write a blog that incorporates and combines your interests.
- Focus your marketing efforts on your niche. Clearly and consistently communicate your message.

YOGIER THAN THOU

Not all yoga classes are the same. For example, some teachers like to focus on what I call *woo woo* (unscientific theories communicated as truth). This may include astrology, the use of crystals, and the like. There is nothing wrong with believing in these things and incorporating them into your yoga class as long as you clearly communicate what your class is about and seek others who are interested in those same things.

When I was in my 20s living in West Hollywood, I would go every Monday night to Yoga on Melrose. Yogi Stu would hand out pot brownies or other edibles and play hip hop and we would all have tea together afterward. It was awesome. But, that type of class is certainly not for everyone. My point being...find your people. Create a tribe of like minded people and you can lead the way.

When not teaching or practicing yoga, my other passion is chess. I have taught beginners the game for many years, but often question if I'm a qualified teacher because I feel I'm not a strong player. However, I know this feeling is akin to how I felt when I first started teaching yoga. The truth is I am a good chess teacher because I am able to convey the nuances of the game in a way that is accessible to those who struggle with learning the basic principles of chess. I consider my ability to make chess accessible to students of all ages to be my specialty. I draw on my patience and utilize visuals and mnemonics to make learning fun and help students make the connections to chess.

I am not trying to sell my services as someone who will "coach" your child to win a tournament or increase rating points, but I will be able to teach you to play and give you the confidence in your ability to learn. That is my niche and recognizing it moved me away from the mindset that I am an imposter and replaced it with the reality that I am providing a service to a specific audience who will benefit from my approach.

Coming back to yoga, I apply this point to help you find what makes you different. What is your strength? What do you bring to the table? In what ways can you help your students access yoga?

CONNECTING WITH YOUR STUDENTS

Forming a connection with your students is the best way to ensure they come to your class week after week. In addition to learning your students' names, here are other ways to form connections.

- When introducing yourself, offer a personal share. When you are vulnerable, you create a connection with your students and give them permission to do the same.
- Be able to read your students. Not all people like burning sage. Not all people are into chakras and

talking about spirituality. Not only know who you are as a teacher, but make sure you know who your students are.

- Keep a list of students who have taken your class. If you keep contact information, you can send a newsletter, invite them to special events, or send a check-in note if you haven't seen them in a while.
- Keep notes about your class and students to track any injuries, conversations, or specific things your students enjoy in class.
- Track how many times your students come to your class.
- Encourage new students to come back. Build long-term relationships with your students, keep them informed about new classes, and offer them discounted passes. Make sure you have promotional materials to hand out, which includes your website and business contact details.
- Get reviews and testimonials. If you see a student who is benefiting from your lessons, ask him/her to give you a review on social media or a short testimonial that you can put on your website.

ATTRACTING YOUR STUDENTS

One reason people may not be coming to your class is because they don't know about it. Your friends and family may not even know when you teach. You need to remember, just because yoga is on your mind 24/7, it isn't on everyone's mind. You know those algorithms that social media uses to get your attention? Well just because you are flooded with yoga overload, doesn't mean everyone else is too.

To help students find you, try these simply to employ methods:

- Attend classes at other studios.

Make friends, start conversations, and let people know you teach yoga too. Create a flyer and post it on bulletin boards, car windshields, and in mailboxes. Drop flyers off with the concierge at area hotels and ask local businesses if they will distribute. Include handouts that show your schedule of drop-in classes. Place some in the waiting rooms of offices that may attract like minded individuals such as chiropractors, massage therapists, or health stores.

- Offer a free yoga workshop.

If you are a beginning teacher and feel reluctant to charge, you may be more comfortable gaining experience by teaching for free or donation. Offer to give a free workshop to organizations such as women's groups, school PTAs, AA meetings, or church groups. The key to successfully attracting students that resonate with your teaching lies in marketing your uniqueness as a teacher.

Some teachers want to teach to as many people as possible, or travel to different places to teach. Other yoga teachers are content with teaching at their local studio to the same small group of students.

Private lessons, special events, retreats . . . These are all ways to build your student following, make more money than you're typically paid per class at a studio, and diversify your teaching portfolio.

Yoga retreats and special events, such as weekend workshops or hosting a themed class, are also excellent ways to create a name for yourself.

What's most important as a new instructor is to begin teaching as soon as possible. The more you teach, the more confident you'll become.

. . .

THE DREADED NUMBERS

So, you got a job and are teaching. Congratulations! You feel confident in your ability and you receive positive feedback about your class. So why are your attendance numbers still low?

It's normal for a new class to take 3-6 months to attract a following. Consider how long you have been in that teaching slot with a low number of students. Is the class size low because you only recently started teaching in that time slot? Or have you been in that slot for over 3-6 months with no luck?

If you've been at it for awhile in this slot, but still experiencing low turnout, it may have nothing to do with your teaching ability. It could be that the time is an off peak time or the time slot is competing with other similar, more well established classes.

Ask yourself if your attendance is better during other times or other formats that you teach. The reason for low numbers may simply be an undesirable time slot.

However, if all of your classes are resulting in low numbers of students, it's time to look at what you can do to improve. Consider getting honest feedback from another teacher. Be open to listening to what your studio manager says about your teaching, if they have received feedback about you.

By focusing your efforts on trying to make your class serve your students, you will find your niche and your following.

CHAPTER SEVENTEEN

MAKING A LIVING

DO you know why you want to teach yoga? If you want to make money doing something you love like yoga, you need to be creative. The amount of time you spend prepping, preparing, self-educating, and teaching can be immense. Before you can make a living teaching yoga, you need to evaluate how much time you're spending in the pursuit. To be successful, you must have a clear grasp of *why* you teach and *how* you go about it.

How long were you looking up specific poses on the internet? How long did it take to develop your playlist? How many times did you practice your sequence? How long did it take you to drive to and from class? How long did it take you to email potential students, collect money, send flyers?

In reality, teaching a one-hour class could take up to eight hours of your time. This is an investment in time and energy. Figure this in when you plan what to charge for a class.

Tapping into a Market

According to an article in the Yoga Baron, 361 yoga studio owners from 2017 to 2019 participated in a survey asking what times and days their studio was busiest. They found Monday to be the busiest day and late afternoons to be the busiest times.

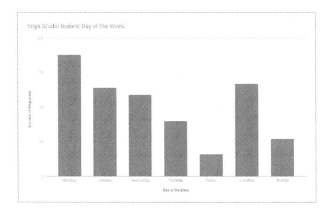

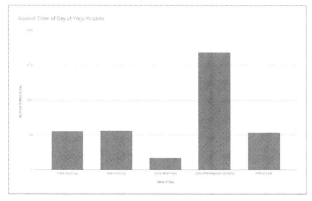

These figures can be used to help make sense of the best way to market your classes. It appears that working people come to classes directly after work.

Perhaps you capitalize on this market and approach large businesses and offer to teach classes on their work site. The benefit for employees would be not worrying about getting to class on time or crowds.

Markets Beyond Yoga Studios

What type of environment do you want to teach in? To answer this, refer back to your yoga goals. The variety of setting include:

- Corporate
- Private
- Schools
- Studios
- Gyms

As with everything, there are pros and cons to each situation. When deciding on the environment you want to teach in, it may be helpful to weigh your options.

Large Studio

Pros:

- Regular schedule
- Many opportunities to teach
- Often includes a free membership and other perks like retail discounts
- Brand name credibility
- Ongoing training and learning opportunities
- No overhead

Cons:

- Workplace politics
- Limited mentoring
- The priority is profit
- Staff is disposable
- Lesser pay
- Less autonomy

GYM CHAIN
Pros:

- You can market to an already active and potential student base.

Cons:

- Students tend to show up late and leave early.
- Yoga is an afterthought to other fitness priorities.
- Lighting and music may be fixed.

LOCAL BUSINESSES
Pros:

- The pay and perks for teaching at a company or large organization can be higher.
- People will be more inclined to attend with co-workers.

Cons:

- The location could vary from being a huge fitness room to a conference or lunch room with distractions.
- You will be responsible for bringing any props and music.
- Students may try out class and drop out. They are less invested and have less time due to work related duties and distractions.

BOUTIQUE STUDIO:
Pros:

- You will have a committed student base. The students tend to be more open minded.

Cons:

- You will be responsible for finding your own students and building your following.
- The pay tends to be lower and based on per student or donation only.
- You may even have to "pay to play," meaning pay the studio a rental fee.

SELF EMPLOYED PRIVATES:
Pros:

- You are in control and can tailor your class any way you see fit.
- You teach in a private setting and have leverage to set a higher rate.

Cons:

- Financial responsibility falls on you.
- If you are teaching in other people's homes, you do not have control of your environment (dogs, noise, privacy, interruptions).

ONLINE:
Pros:

- You will be able to record your classes, which can help you refine your teaching.
- You can teach to a limitless audience.
- Little overhead.
- You can teach anywhere.

Cons:

- Less connection with students.
- Potential for tech issues.

MARKETING

If you are building a yoga business or building your student base, you have to take marketing into account. How you present yourself and your services will make the difference between making money or spinning your wheels wondering why you are not getting students.

You need a clear idea of your yoga teaching goals and a clear plan on how to get there. Before you start marketing, teach as much as possible to determine your market.

When you have a niche market, you can start building your brand. I am not going to go into the ins and outs of marketing your business because you can buy books on that or hire people to help you. But here are some essentials to keep in mind.

BUSINESS NECESSITIES:

- Business Cards
- Website
- Email Address
- Yoga Resume/Bio
- Informational Flyer
- Yoga Insurance

OPTIONAL BUSINESS ADD-ONS:

- Personal Logo and Tagline
- YouTube Channel (make sure to only use royalty free music or obtain necessary licenses).
- Social Media (Instagram, Facebook, Facebook Group, Pinterest, SnapChat, Twitter)
- Yoga Alliance membership
- Contact Database System
- Yoga Studio Music License

MUSIC DURING CLASS

If you teach yoga in a public class, it falls under the definition of a "public performance." The music you play requires a licensing fee paid to one of the performance rights organizations (BMI, ASCAP and SESAC). Whether you are teaching a class in a public park or at a busy studio, playing music for an online class, or using your own CDs are all actions that require a license.

There is a special Yoga Studio Music License that can be obtained directly with each organization or you can sign up through Yoga Alliance and get a discount.

Subscriptions to royalty free music via a streaming service that offers music with a license for public performance is available through YogiTunes and SiriusXM. If you plan to use Spotify or Pandora playlists in your yoga classes, you must obtain the appropriate business license to cover public performances. These include Spotify Business - Soundtrack Your Brand and Pandora Business - Mood Media. If you have any questions regarding required insurance or licensing, please consult a lawyer.

Whereas the music license may be necessary, in my opinion, if you know you are not interested in teaching online, don't waste your time and energy purchasing equipment and software to create

YouTube videos. It is nice to have as an added value, but it is not necessary across the board.

REACHING YOUR AUDIENCE

What is necessary, is knowing your audience and being able to reach them. In terms of social media, remember you want to connect to students. It's not necessary to spend a lot of energy following other yoga teachers. You want to cater to your student. Review previous chapters to determine your speciality and use that to find your students.

Have you ever had a job where there was no job description and you created it on the fly? Think of this exercise in the same manner. Create your job description by focusing on a need within your perspective student. This is how you want to think about finding a niche.

BE CREATIVE

I cannot stress enough... you want to think creatively. Try to find people who may have never tried yoga before. You might reach out to fire or police stations to offer a class to first responders to ease stress. Maybe you target health workers at treatment centers. These are all undiscovered niches.

Utilize what you are good at and enjoy and combine it with a need someone has. If you have friends who are MLM (multi-level marketers), consider partnering with them. Multi-Level Marketing is ripe for groups of people who are ready to "buy in". You know the Tupperware, Avon or Arbonne model. Work with the sales rep and offer to teach a free yoga class to anyone who purchases at "parties" as a gift. This is an opportunity to market your services with advertising. If someone does not know what you are offering, they will never become your student. You need to inform people who you are and what you offer.

Do not think of it as selling. You are letting people know who you are and what you can help them with. You can pitch meditation or gentle stretching, helping digestion, healing a broken heart, a singles meet up... the possibilities are endless.

REMIND ME AGAIN... WHY AM I DOING THIS?

If marketing sounds like a lot of work, remember that you probably made a significant investment into your yoga teacher training.

The most basic level is the RYT (Registered Yoga Teacher) 200-hour training course, which typically involves classroom training, hands-on instruction, and a final exam.

The timeline and costs of these courses vary, but through the survey I conducted, a 200-hour course typically runs between $3,000-$5,000. How much time and how many classes will you need to teach to recoup this cost?

Making money may or may not be your main priority. But regardless of what you charge for your services, it is never a good idea to sell yourself short and give it away for free. When you teach free classes, your intention may be to build community and be of service, but what you are actually doing is devaluing your service.

I am all for donating services for fundraising or in order to convert people into paying members or clients, but your free class must have a purpose. When you teach for free, you not only give away your time and service, but also pay out of pocket to teach for free. Remember to consider your gas expense, your time to organize, plan and prepare all cost you something. Time money and energy are spent.

As I mentioned, in addition to teaching yoga, I also teach beginning chess. Once when I was teaching chess, I came upon an opportunity. I have a friend who is a personal chef for a wealthy family. The woman of the house wanted to learn to play chess so she could play with her grandson. My friend asked me if I was interested in teaching this woman. I immediately jumped at the opportunity and told my friend my rate was $30/hour (which is reasonable and fair for beginning chess lessons). However, I neglected to factor in the gas and time for driving. This woman lived in the city and it would take me easily 45 minutes to get there. My friend told me I could not possibly charge so little. He suggested charging for a 2-hour minimum lesson to figure in for driving and suggested charging no less than $150/hour. This seemed ludicrous for beginning chess lessons. However, my friend said this woman would value the lesson more based on the higher rate. He swore that this was a selling point to this women. I took my friend's advice and charged $300 for a 2-hour lesson each week. Guess what? She happily paid it.

I am not suggesting you charge $300 for a yoga lesson. I am merely pointing out that value is subjective. If you do not want to put a price on a lesson, by all means, make it a donation-based class and provide a "suggested donation" amount. Some people will not donate, but some will pay handsomely.

Some teachers obtain their training in India or other retreat locations where courses (and the cost of living) are much cheaper.

Often, students select a training at a studio where they practice and subsequently audition for jobs to teach where they did their training. This is obviously a comfortable transition. You already know the people at the studio and the clientele. You know what the studio is looking for and that you have been professionally trained to work there.

The problem with this is that if your goal is to branch out and become a yoga instructor and not just an employee of a corporate owned studio, you will have to teach in a variety of environments. This will stretch you outside your comfort zone, but as you know, without discomfort, there is no growth!

Some studios pay hourly; some pay based on the number of students you bring in. Some will allow you to use the studio for a rental fee and you can charge your students individual rates. Make sure you know upfront what your compensation will be when applying for jobs and getting offers to teach.

Keep in mind that although your actual teaching time may only be one hour, some studios require you to be there 30 minutes before class to sign students in, as well as 30 minutes afterwards to close up shop. You also should figure in time and gas costs to get to/from studio as well as the time and energy it takes to prepare a sequence and playlist. Most teachers I know can lose hours of time building the "perfect playlist". We call it falling down the Spotify rabbit hole. The more you fall, the more time and money falls away with you.

CAN I EARN A LIVING?

Deciding how to structure your pay rate often depends on where you teach. Most studios offer teachers a flat rate per class. The rate is the same regardless of how many students reserve or show up for class. Flat rates can vary in range from $15 per class on the low end to upwards of $50 per class on the high end.

Other studios will pay a flat rate as a base pay and a bonus per head rate as an incentive for teachers to grow their class size. Often the flat rate applies to a certain number of students and then as the number grows, the teacher will receive additional payment for each student over the base number.

Some studios do not pay teachers a flat rate at all. The studio allows the teacher access to the studio and marketing efforts. In exchange, they get a portion of the student fee or charge the teacher for the rental space. In this situation, the teacher decides what to charge the student. Again, this arrangement requires teachers to seek out students and build their following or they will actually lose money.

TEACHING IN A TRADITIONAL STUDIO SETTING OR GYM IS NOT an instructor's only option. Once you have found your niche and teaching style, you will be able to widen your potential teaching opportunities.

In fact, if you are looking to make money as a full time yoga instructor and do not want to burn out or have little energy for your own teaching practice, stepping out of the studio and branching out into other yoga related areas will be your most viable and lucrative option.

CUSTOMIZE YOUR TEACHING TO YOUR INTERESTS

If you are already an avid surfer and you teach yoga, you can customize yoga for the surfer and focus on balance, strength, and core development. You can make it a restorative class and work on muscles that are commonly used and injured due to surfing motion. You can keep your intentions related to surf life.

Here are some other creative teaching options to consider:

- Businesses that have space for a yoga class. Maybe approach restaurants, wineries and bars that have a live music area and pitch a yoga and tasting class.
- Consider venues that lend themselves to reflection such as museums, libraries, gardens, and other community spaces.
- Think of gatherings that bring people together such as bridal showers, reunions, graduations, and birthday celebrations.
- Corporate venues such as banks, healthcare, insurance, and financial industries are viable marketing targets. In fact, teaching in a corporate setting can be extremely lucrative because these businesses often have more budget to spend on wellness.
- Non-profit charity tie-ins and fundraisers

THE MAIN FOCUS OF THIS BOOK IS HOW TO TEACH WITH confidence. You may be asking yourself, "Why am I reading about yoga business?" Well, because if you dream it, you can make it possible.

If you do not like the idea of marketing your business, you could hire someone to help you. This could be money well spent. However, you don't need to spend more money on additional training to become a better yoga instructor. With practice, you will become a better yoga instructor. However, to make money at yoga and to find students to teach yoga to, you need to become a savvy marketer and more specialized.

My strength is in marketing and writing, so here I am writing about one of my favorite topics and favorite things to do... Yoga. Whether you teach in person or online, in a corporate environment or at a gym, the secret is to determine what exactly you are good at and like doing and figure out how to incorporate yoga into it. This is the difference between having to choose between making money or doing what you love. How about making money doing what you love?!

This is how I fell into the world of chess and now am paid to teach it. I actually fell into the chess world quite by accident. I saw how amazing chess was and how it was something that was referenced in every area of life. I decided I would put together a program and contact mental health and treatment facilities and "sell" a chess program for the residents. I had never worked in this setting before.

But guess what? I was brought on at a treatment center and I gained my hours as I studied for my CADC (Certified Alcohol and Drug Counselor) license. Finding your niche will not only help you in regard to a career in yoga, but will help you in regard to carving your place out in life.

. . .

Marketing Considerations - Your Privacy

In today's social media world, there are really only two options. Keeping your private life completely private or making your private life, public and completely transparent. There really is no in between.

If you like your privacy, just know you will have to take measures to keep your social media for your yoga business separate from your personal social media. That means setting up two separate profiles for the social media channels you plan to use and setting your personal pages to private. The other option is being totally transparent.

If you are okay with transparency, remember that means being okay that your students can find your address and whether you are married, what day job you have, what extra-curricular activities you partake in and what groups you are affiliated with.

This is totally a personal choice. For me, it seems like too much work to try to keep my lives separate. I find that the approach, "This is who I am, take it or leave it," works for me. But I totally understand the desire for privacy.

It all depends on what your yoga goals are when you decide how much to invest in your yoga business. If you are going to maintain a business presence, then a couple of considerations are essential:

1. Consistent Posting – Whether you are posting YouTube videos, a blog, or Instagram photos, you must keep this up to maintain an active presence.
2. Follow Up - If you receive requests and comments, make sure that you follow up to each and every message in a timely manner.
3. Be An Example – Praise and acknowledge others publicly. Keep negative opinions and retorts to yourself. Never bad talk other instructors or business practices or engage in trolling behavior.

Under Promise and Over Deliver

When you finish yoga teacher training and get hired with a corporate studio, you will get asked to sub classes. Beware. There is a saying, "Under promise and over deliver."

Pros of Subbing

- Gain teaching experience
- Great opportunity to try out new sequences and playlists
- No commitment to a time slot
- Feels good to help others out and build network of peers
- Opportunity to meet students that aren't available for your regular time slot

Cons of Subbing

- Comparisons to "regular" teacher
- More challenging to connect with students
- Unable to build a solid student base
- You become forgettable

When you are always ready and eager to pitch in, teachers and the studio will rely on this and it is more difficult to back out. "Don't worry, ask Julie..." You also may become resentful when no one seems to step up in your time of need.

It is totally okay to decline. You do not need to share your reason. You do not need to provide an excuse. You do not need to apologize. You can always offer an exchange, trade, or negotiate something else so that you are benefiting as well. If you like to sub and like getting the experience, then you are getting something out of it. But do not think Karma is going to come into play. This is a business and corporate yoga studios are there to make money.

Never think you are irreplaceable... in the workplace, that is. Do not let this concept define who you are and your identity and self-worth. I had to learn the hard way from years of experience in the workplace that you are always replaceable in the workplace, but that does not mean you are replaceable as a person.

CHAPTER EIGHTEEN

SVADHYAYA – SELF STUDY

EVERY TEACHER IS A STUDENT. Every student is a teacher.

When you are in the role of yoga teacher, you have a special opportunity to influence and inspire as well as the power to educate and guide others toward health. Do not take this role lightly. The best bit of advice I can give you is, "Plant seeds and lead by example."

To lead, you must be clear on who you are and what you have to offer. In short, you must always take part in self-study. This chapter includes a highly comprehensive list of self-study and self-reflection exercises.

There are no "right" answers to these questions. There is only the right answer for you. The purpose is to notice and reflect on your true feelings without judgment.

Take your time and reflect on the following questions to help guide you toward your reason for wanting to teach yoga, what you will offer your students, and most importantly, what it is that makes you uniquely yourself.

Ask Yourself...

Why Do I Practice Yoga?

Start to notice what you are drawn to as a student. If you know what it is that you love about yoga, you will naturally be able to weave it into your classes. Common answers may be to improve your health, calm your mind, or even to practice with like-minded individuals.

Why Do I Want to Teach Yoga?

Just as there are a number of reasons why people practice, there are a many things that inspire people to teach. Teaching yoga requires a different skill set from practicing yoga. Being able to master postures perfectly is not a requirement of the job. Teaching is a skill that requires patience and leadership. It is more important to be able to connect, be genuine, and communicate effectively than it is to be able to twist yourself into bound lotus pose.

Make sure that it is not just the love of yoga that drives you to teach, but also the love of educating and leading others that propels you to the job.

What is My Yoga Teaching Style?

Your personal style is not the brand of leggings you wear. Your yoga teaching style is how you guide your students through a sequence. Are you fun and silly? Are you serious and focused Are you spiritual and meditative? Are you pragmatic and drawn to the anatomy of the postures?

Knowing who you are and what you have to offer is the key to developing your teaching style. No two people can teach the same class. Everyone has a personal teaching style and the more you are able to pinpoint what it is that makes you unique, the more you can develop your class to showcase your personal style. This is the first step in finding your niche and your fanbase.

Once you determine your strengths and your proclivities, you can find your unique voice and natural abilities to make you a more authentic teacher. When you try to add too many different aspects into your class, you will come across as inauthentic. It is best to teach what motivates and inspires you.

I like to use anatomy cues to help students make the connection between how our internal systems work through breath. Safety is paramount for me. I like to bring students' attention to foot placement, warming up the body, and protecting the lower back, to name a few. Yet, I also like to add silliness and a sense of play because I think it gives students permission to laugh and find joy in their practice. I like to unite students and use a lot of language and intention to support community, shared experiences, and belonging.

Another teacher may focus more on improvement and building strength. This teacher may use more encouraging language to help students advance or find their edge and focus on pushing limits.

Neither approach is wrong. Your style of teaching will resonate with a population of students and those students are your tribe. Greet your students with a smile; give them a great class; and, remember their name. They will become your people.

WHAT IS MY STUDIO'S STYLE?

Teaching at a studio where you took training might not support your desire to find your own voice and style. Although a love of yoga may have first inspired your studio owners, they must focus on their profit margin in order to run a successful business. To accomplish this, they have found a formula that works. The trick is to work within their guidelines while finding your unique style. You must allow enough individuality to shine through to set you apart from the robotic, canned teachers that often get churned out from corporate yoga studios.

CHAPTER NINETEEN

SELF-REFLECTION EXERCISES

NOW THAT YOU'VE had an opportunity to answer some generalized questions about your yoga teaching goals, it's time to dig deeper.

The following self-reflection exercises are designed to help you determine your yoga niche and what you hope to achieve by teaching yoga.

———

DO YOU PREFER TO WORK ALONE OR WITH A GROUP? ONE ON ONE OR IN A BUSY ENVIRONMENT?

This will help you narrow down if you might be better suited for privates or large group classes and retreats.

DO YOU PREFER TO BE THE GUEST OR HOST OF A PARTY?

Your answer can give insight into your interest level to teach versus practice.

. . .

ARE YOU COMFORTABLE TAKING RISKS?

This can help you determine whether you want to work for yourself or might be better suited working for someone else.

WHAT HAS TO HAPPEN BEFORE YOUR "REAL" LIFE STARTS?

This is a pretty deep question, but it's effective to understand what might be standing in the way of your goals.

WHAT ACTIVITIES DO YOU AVOID?

This question helps you see patterns and fears that may sabotage your success.

WHAT IS YOUR FAVORITE GENRE?

Consider the books you read, shows you watch, or podcasts you listen to. A love of mysteries may mean you like problem solving. The genres you gravitate toward may translate into class themes and intentions.

DO YOU HAVE MORE ENERGY IN THE MORNING OR EVENING?

This can help you plan when to schedule classes so you are at your best.

WHAT IS MORE IMPORTANT TO YOU... SAVING TIME OR SAVING MONEY?

I threw this question in because it can provide some insight as to how to plan and structure your classes.

WHAT DO YOU LOOK FOR IN A YOGA TEACHER?

Consider your three favorite yoga or other group fitness teachers. What do you like about them as teachers or their classes? What qualities do they all have in common? Think of a teacher that you do not care for. What do they do or not do that turns you off? Can you also find something positive about this teacher's class?

WHAT ASPECT OF YOGA DO YOU THINK IS YOUR STRENGTH?

If money wasn't a factor, what would you be doing right now? This question is always a good one to determine your intention for some of the decisions you make. Maybe you will find that teaching yoga is not something you want to do as a profession.

WHAT TYPES OF THINGS DO YOU LOSE PATIENCE OVER?

Teaching of any kind requires a great deal of patience. Being clear on what your triggers are will also help you determine your ideal teaching environment.

WHAT INSPIRES YOU?

Consider what are you doing and who are you with when you feel inspired.

ARE THERE POSTURES YOU AVOID?

Why? Can you find a modification? In contrast, think of the postures and types of yoga you most enjoy (inversions, meditation, flow, stretch, etc.).

WHAT DO YOU WANT YOUR STUDENTS TO LEARN IN YOUR CLASS?

How do you want your students to feel after class? What do students say about your class? Do students leave you reviews? Think about your personal experiences off the mat and how sharing these experiences could help others succeed. What do you want your yoga legacy to be?

WHERE DO YOU HOPE TO TEACH?

Think of different environments where you might teach (parks, schools, etc.) and the populations you may teach to (kids, pregnant women, young adults, seniors). What was your experience? What did you like or not like about teaching to this population?

WHAT ARE YOU GOOD AT?

Consider skills beyond yoga. You could answer with cooking, chess, crafts. Think of your personal interests. How can you add yoga to this interest?

HOW DO YOU FEEL AFTER A "GOOD" CLASS?

Does the theme or intention affect how you feel? Is it the poses or the cues? What can you emulate from your favorite teachers and classes to incorporate into your own teaching?

COMPLETE THIS SENTENCE...
I TEACH BECAUSE I WANT STUDENTS TO...

———————

CORE VALUES

Following are a list of basic core values. Rate the values

according to numbers 1-5 below and when finished, notice your priorities.

1. Very Important
2. Important
3. Somewhat Important,
4. Not Important
5. Definitely Not Important

Fairness	Honesty	Courage
Integrity	Forgiveness	Peace
Challenge	Self-Respect	Self-Acceptance
Knowledge	Adventure	Creativity
Personal Growth	Belonging	Inner Harmony
Spiritual Growth	Diplomacy	Teamwork
Helpfulness	Friendship	Communication
Respect	Security	Stability
Neatness	Self-Control	Perseverance
Rationality	Health	Pleasure
Play	Excellence	Prosperity
Family	Appearance	Intimacy
Beauty	Community	Competence
Achievement	God	Intellectual Status
Recognition	Authority	Competition
Persistence	Wisdom	Tradition

PERSONAL BRAND

Following is a selection of words that will help formulate your personal brand and the traits that represent you.

Circle the words below that resonate with you.

Next, group similar traits together and create a maximum of five groupings.

Finally, select one word from each grouping that best describes you.

Able	Brainy	Content	Educated
Accepting	Brave	Confident	Efficient
Accomplished	Bright	Considerate	Empathetic
Active	Busy	Courageous	Encouraging
Adaptable	Calm	Courteous	Energetic
Admirable	Captivating	Creative	Enthusiastic
Adventurous	Careful	Curious	Excited
Affectionate	Caring	Daring	Expert
Aggressive	Cautious	Decisive	Fair
Ambitious	Challenging	Deep	Faithful
Apologetic	Charismatic	Dependable	Fearless
Appreciative	Charming	Determined	Fierce
Appropriate	Cheerful	Devoted	Flexible
Articulate	Clear-headed	Disciplined	Focused
Assertive	Clever	Discreet	Forgiving
Attentive	Colorful	Down to Earth	Fortunate
Aware	Compassionate	Dynamic	Fresh
Balanced	Concerned	Eager	Friendly
Bold	Conciliatory	Easygoing	Funny

Generous	Insightful	Optimistic	Safe
Gentle	Intelligent	Organized	Satisfied
Goofy	Kind	Patient	Self-Directed
Graceful	Leader	Peaceful	Sensitive
Gracious	Listener	Polite	Serious
Grateful	Lively	Popular	Silly
Happy	Loving	Positive	Skilled
Hardworking	Loyal	Practical	Sly
Healthy	Lucky	Proud	Smart
Helpful	Mature	Quick	Strict
Honest	Meticulous	Quiet	Strong
Honorable	Moderate	Rational	Sweet
Hopeful	Modest	Realistic	Tactful
Humble	Motivated	Reliable	Talented
Imaginative	Mysterious	Relaxed	Thankful
Impartial	Nervous	Religious	Thoughtful
Independent	Nice	Resilient	Trusting
Industrious	Nurturing	Respectful	Trustworthy
Innovative	Open Minded	Responsible	Warm

What five words most resonate with you? These are the traits that will help you narrow your teaching style and develop your niche.

WHY YOGA?

What attracts you to the practice of yoga (ie: anatomy, arm

balances, balancing, emotional release)? Rate the items below in order of preference: 4-favorite, 3-like, 2-no preference, 1-avoid at all costs

Arm Balances

Back Bends

Balancing

Binds

Breath Work

Core Work

Flow

Forward Folds

Gentle Stretch

Holds

Inversions

Props

GOAL SETTING

The following questions will require deep reflection. Your answers may change and evolve over time, but if you give these questions thoughtful consideration, you may find that you can refocus your efforts to better move toward your goals.

ASK YOURSELF...

- What three activities make me lose time?

- What is one thing that I want to accomplish in this life?
- Do I believe that I am capable?
- Do I believe I will do what is necessary to accomplish my goals? Why or why not?
- What previous experience/education will help me accomplish my goals?
- What is standing in my way?
- How will my life look once I accomplish my goals?
- What kind of people do I want to have around me?
- What kind of mark do I want to make?
- What are the things I ruminate most on and often lose sleep over?
- What activities or things do I do out of obligation?
- What things do I do that make a difference?
- What things do I do to feed my ego?
- What are things I do for fun and fulfillment?
- What do I sacrifice?

Once you determine what it is that you want to accomplish, every time you are faced with a decision to make, ask yourself if this moves you toward your goalS or away from them?

SELF-EFFICACY

Do you remember reading about self-efficacy, the belief that you have what it takes to be successful? The General Self-Efficacy Scale (GSE) was developed by Matthias Jerusalem and Ralf Schwarzer. The scale is composed of only 8 items, rated on a scale from 1 (strongly disagree) to 5 (strongly agree).

1. I will be able to achieve most of the goals that I set for myself.
2. When facing difficult tasks, I am certain that I will accomplish them.

3. In general, I think that I can obtain outcomes that are important to me.
4. I believe I can succeed at most any endeavor to which I set my mind.
5. I will be able to successfully overcome many challenges.
6. I am confident that I can perform effectively on many different tasks.
7. Compared to other people, I can do most tasks very well.
8. Even when things are tough, I can perform quite well.

Your score is calculated by taking the average of all 8 responses. These range from 1 to 5. The test implies that the higher one's score, the greater the level of self-efficacy.

Rock Star Yogi Exercise

Create your rock star file, also known as the "I am fucking awesome" file. Include notes from friends, coworkers, and students. Anyone and everyone who has recognized you for something you did, said, or are belongs in this file. If you ever feel incompetent or insecure, come back to this file and remind yourself that you rock.

Own Your Accomplishments

A common trait that many of us share is trying to explain away our successes by saying things like, "It was just luck," or "I only was successful because of X." I think our tendency is to downplay our successes for fear of self-promoting, bragging, or looking arrogant. Instead of owning our success, we make ourselves look small. The more we do this, the smaller we make ourselves feel. Try to own the role you played in your success. Practice saying these words out loud: "I'm proud of what I've accomplished."

. . .

Visualize your success

Visualize your limitless potential and imagine what it feels like to feel confident and capable. If you can visualize it, you can train your brain. To believe is to achieve.

Get Over Yourself

When you doubt yourself and feel like an imposter, just stop and ask yourself, "Do I really believe that everyone else is a complete idiot and I have them all fooled?" Do not disrespect your friends, family, employers, students, or audience. If they hired you and believed in you, then maybe you should believe in yourself too!

Looking Forward

There is evidence that imagining our best possible self can help to improve optimism and motivation for change. Look forward and visualize your future success.

- What are you doing?
- Can you describe the environment you are in?
- What does your day look like?
- Can you envision the people who surround you?

Looking Back

So often, we are focused on what is next or planning for our future, we forget to take a look back and see how far we have come. When we look back on our lives, it is easy to gloss over all the things that have gone well. Take a look back and complete the following exercises:

- List all of your accomplishments (big and small).

I do not care if it is winning a spelling bee in 3rd grade, graduating high school, or asking someone out on a date.

- Describe a great day you enjoyed. What made this day feel special?
- Name a challenge that you overcame.
- List three of the best compliments you have ever received. Why did they mean so much to you?

Writing Your Bio

As the previous reflection exercises help to determine your niche, goals, and beliefs, it's now time to write your yoga bio. This bio will be used in marketing materials, your website, and often called upon by your employers.

Although the exercises you've completed will help you create a bio that is truly reflective of who you are, you must remember to include the nuts and bolts of a resume or bio. This includes:

- Your Yoga Practice: How many years you have been practicing?
- Your Yoga Training: What discipline is your training (certifications)in? Where did you train and receive your certification?
- Work Experience: What is your practical experience?
- Teaching Style: What is your approach to yoga? Do you combine various disciplines (ie: Hatha, Vinyasa, Ashtanga, Iyengar, Kundalini, Restorative, or Yin)?

A yoga bio can be written in either 1st person or 3rd person. I suggest you write one of each so that they are on hand and appropriate for whomever requests it.

You can use the following template to help you start.

My name is Jen Vallens. I completed my yoga training with CorePower Yoga and have been teaching power style yoga for four years. I love to teach new students in a playful way to explore the mind/body connection. I incorporate fun and familiar music in my classes to help students find natural movement in their bodies. I love yoga because it helps me get in touch with the child within. My classes leave students feeling free in their bodies and their minds.

You Found Yourself!

Discovering your niche and personal style is the first step to attract students to your classes, retreats, workshops, and wherever else you might teach. It's also how you develop your personal brand.

It all begins with YOU. How you see the world, your point of views, your life experiences. But it does not stop there. Your niche extends into how you interact with your students, how you teach your classes, and eventually, how you market to your students.

Business Marketing Exercise

Think of as many activities and vocations you can that would benefit from yoga. Here are just a few examples:

- Yoga and Sports
- Yoga and Chess
- Yoga and Recovery
- Yoga and Wine
- Yoga and Travel
- Yoga and Vegan Cooking

- Yoga and Rock Climbing
- Yoga and Surfing
- Yoga and Skydiving
- Yoga and Mountain Biking
- Yoga and Swimming
- Yoga and Kids
- Yoga and the Busy Professional
- Yoga and Mom
- Yoga and Grandma
- Yoga and Girl Scouts
- Yoga and Adventure Guides
- Yoga and Babies
- Yoga and Moms-To-Be

In addition to combining vocations with yoga, you can think of specific audiences that might benefit from yoga for the purpose of fitness, therapy, mindfulness, movement, sports, trauma, or healing. Below are examples of yoga for specific audiences:

- Gentle Yoga and Meditation for MS
- Chair Yoga for Seniors
- Team Building Yoga for Corporate Retreats
- Restorative Yoga for Rock Climbers
- Yoga for Group Homes or Foster Children
- Yoga for Kids with Autism
- At home Yoga for New Mom and Baby
- Yoga for the Inspired Poet
- Partner Yoga for Twins
- Inversions to Calm the Active Brain
- Yoga and Guided Meditation for the last trimester of pregnancy
- Dating and Yoga... Yoga for Singles, Yoga for Jewish Singles, Yoga for Muslims, Yoga for Women

Entrepreneurs, Yoga for Widows, Yoga for the newly divorced
- Even Yoga for Stamp Collectors

You get the idea. There are an infinite number of ways you can market yourself and market yoga. After completing these exercises, wait a few days and then look at your answers again.

Do you see any patterns? Does anything you wrote jump out to you? Highlight it and wait another few days to look at it again. I know you will find the path that is right for you and develop your ability to teach with confidence.

EPILOGUE

WHAT DID you discover about yourself in the course of this book and its exercises? This book was designed to be akin to a good yoga class. That is, a good yoga class is like a journey. We arrive one way, set an intention, get into our practice, slow down, and leave transformed.

My hope for you is that you discover something new about yourself that you can bring to your students, and in turn, help them with their journey. My intention for writing this book is to set you up for success so that you may have a positive yoga teaching journey. As in a yoga class, allow the intention to carry you from beginning to end. Let's do one last visualization exercise to close out this book.

I read somewhere that the only person you need to impress is your 5-year-old self and your 85-year-old self. After reading this, close your eyes and imagine for a moment you are a small child. Think back to a time when you felt scared, lonely, sad, or disappointed. Maybe your parent didn't show up when they said they would, or you got sick and could not go to Disneyland.

Once you have the image, I want you to now imagine yourself at your current age knocking on the door of younger you. I want you to sit with your younger self and give yourself a hug. I want you to say all the things you needed to hear when you were this small child. I want you to tell your younger self how strong and amazing he/she is and all the wonderful things that he/she has to look forward to. Start to tell him/her about all the things that he/she is going to do and be proud of. Give him/her a big hug and say good-bye. Let him/her know that you will always be a guide and show the way.

Now I want you to imagine you are the age you are now and you get a knock on the door and it is 85-year-old you. I want you to tell your older, wiser self all the worries and fears you are feeling. I want you to tell yourself everything that is making you anxious and standing in your way. I want you to imagine that your 85-year-old self reaches out, gives you a hug, and says, "I love you. Thank you for being with me all these years. Thank you for taking care of my body and my mind and being such a good friend to me. You are beautiful and you matter. So please stop worrying about others and think of me once in awhile."

Happy teaching. Happy learning. Remember to find balance within yourself as a yoga teacher and yoga student, as we are all both.

WORKSHEETS & TEMPLATES

THEME _____   PEAK POSTURE: _____   PLAYLIST: _____

STARTING POSE: _____

SUN B   1 time slow/ 2 times flow

WARM UPS

SUN A   1 time slow/ 2 times flow

Use this worksheet to help design your warm-up, Sun A and
Sun B flow.

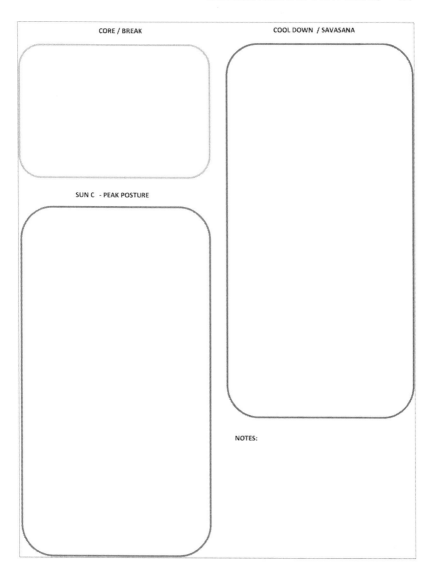

CORE / BREAK

COOL DOWN / SAVASANA

SUN C - PEAK POSTURE

NOTES:

In the next example, you can see how I have used downward facing dog and transitioned into warrior 2, and then warrior 2 to chaturanga. You can mix and match these same mini blocks to create nine different sequences.

Sun B Sequence

Using the same Peak and the same basic framework

Mini Block 1:

Starting with Right Leg High

Ending with Warrior 2

Mini Block 2:

Starting with Warrior 2

Ending with Chaturanga

Each Mini Block can be repeated with adding in some variations:

- Knee to Nose
- Holding the squat
- Adding pulses
- Add a twist or bind
- Add a Baby Back Bend
- Add Eagle Arm Crunches
- Add in Double Lunge

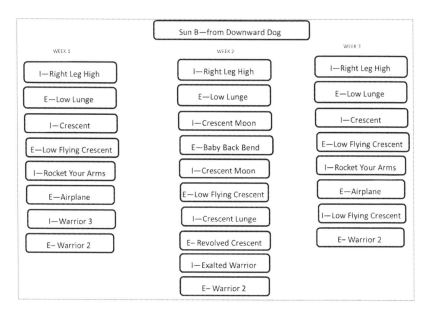

Sun B—from Downward Dog

WEEK 1

- I—Right Leg High
- E—Low Lunge
- I—Crescent
- E—Low Flying Crescent
- I—Rocket Your Arms
- E—Airplane
- I—Warrior 3
- E— Warrior 2

WEEK 2

- I—Right Leg High
- E—Low Lunge
- I—Crescent Moon
- E—Baby Back Bend
- I—Crescent Moon
- E—Low Flying Crescent
- I—Crescent Lunge
- E— Revolved Crescent
- I—Exalted Warrior
- E— Warrior 2

WEEK 3

- I—Right Leg High
- E—Low Lunge
- I—Crescent
- E—Low Flying Crescent
- I—Rocket Your Arms
- E—Airplane
- I—Low Flying Crescent
- E— Warrior 2

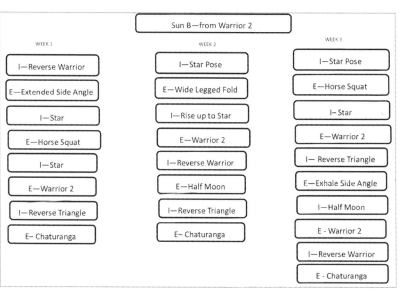

Sun B—from Warrior 2

WEEK 1

- I—Reverse Warrior
- E—Extended Side Angle
- I—Star
- E—Horse Squat
- I—Star
- E—Warrior 2
- I—Reverse Triangle
- E— Chaturanga

WEEK 2

- I—Star Pose
- E—Wide Legged Fold
- I—Rise up to Star
- E—Warrior 2
- I—Reverse Warrior
- E—Half Moon
- I—Reverse Triangle
- E— Chaturanga

WEEK 3

- I—Star Pose
- E—Horse Squat
- I- Star
- E—Warrior 2
- I— Reverse Triangle
- E—Exhale Side Angle
- I—Half Moon
- E - Warrior 2
- I—Reverse Warrior
- E - Chaturanga

REFERENCES

Adele, D. (2009). *The Yamas & Niyamas: Exploring Yoga's Ethical Practice* (4008 1st ed.). On-Word Bound Books.

Awosika, A. (2017). *You 2.0: Stop Feeling Stuck, Reinvent Yourself, and Become a Brand New You - Master the Art of Personal Transformation.* CreateSpace Independent Publishing Platform.

Baptiste, B. (2003). *Journey Into Power: Journey Into Power* (Reprint ed.). Atria Books.

Bergland, C. (2008). *The Athlete's Way: Training Your Mind and Body to Experience the Joy of Exercise* (1st ed.). St. Martin's Griffin.

Clark, B., & Grilley, P. (2016). *Your Body, Your Yoga: Learn Alignment Cues That Are Skillful, Safe, and Best Suited To You* (1st ed.). Wild Strawberry Productions.

Clear, J. (2021). *Atomic Habits.* Random House.

Coco. (n.d.). *Pros and Cons of Yoga Sequence Builders.* Https://Swagtail.Com/. https://swagtail.com/yoga-sequence-builders/

Corrigendum. (2017). *Bulletin of the World Health Organization,* 95(1), 81. https://doi.org/10.2471/blt.17.100117

Cuddy, [Ted Talk]. (2012, January 6). *Body Language* [Video].

YouTube. https://www.ted.com/talks/amy_cuddy_your_body_language_may_shape_who_you_are?language=en

der Kolk, V. B., MD. (2015). *The Body Keeps the Score: Brain, Mind, and Body in the Healing of Trauma* (Reprint ed.). Penguin Books.

Divello, S. (2021). *Where in the Om Am I? by Sara Divello* (2013-03-05). Worcester Square Press.

Dyer. (2016). *Yoga Guide Teach Yourself Yoga at Home* [E-book]. Che Dyer.

Edition, S. (2020). *SUMMARY - The Six Pillars of Self-Esteem by Nathaniel Branden*. Independently published.

Evrard. (2020). *The Sequencing Bible*. Eleanor Evrard.

Gopiao, J. (2016, January 12). *6 Yoga Music Licensing Tips*. LawInc. https://www.lawinc.com/yoga-music-licensing-tips

Hagan. (2019). *A New Yoga Teacher's Guide to Yoga Class Creation* [E-book].

Helmstetter, S. (2019). *Negative Self-Talk and How to Change It*. Park Avenue Press.

Hunt, N. (2019). *A Simple Guide For New Yoga Teachers: Complete With Tips, Poses, and Outlines For Planning Classes*. Excel Avenue Press.

Ippoliti, A., & Smith, T. (2016). *The Art and Business of Teaching Yoga: The Yoga Professional's Guide to a Fulfilling Career* (Illustrated ed.). New World Library.

Ipsos Public Affairs, Yoga Journal, & Yoga Alliance. (2016, January). *Yoga in America Study*. www.Yogaalliance.Org

J. (2018, April 16). *How She Earned 6K in One Year*. Josh Loe. https://www.joshloe.com/2018/04/16/how-she-earned-6k-in-one-year/

Jones. (2019). *No Prep Inspirational Yoga Plans* [E-book]. Rhonda Jones.

Kinealy, J. (2019). *Field Guide to Teaching Yoga: Overcoming Fears, Rising to Challenges, and Thriving in a Job You Love*. Independently published.

Knight, S. (2017). *You Do You: How to Be Who You Are and Use What You've Got to Get What You Want (A No F*cks Given Guide, 3)* (1st ed.). Little, Brown and Company.

Lasater, J. H. (2020). *Yoga Myths: What You Need to Learn and Unlearn for a Safe and Healthy Yoga Practice* (1st ed.). Shambhala.

Long, R. (2021). *Key Muscles of Yoga Your Guide to Functional Anatomy in Yoga 3RD EDITION* [PB,2009]. published by: as shown.

Mischke-Reeds, M. (2018). *Somatic Psychotherapy Toolbox: 125 Worksheets and Exercises for Trauma & Stress (125 Worksheets and Exercises to Treat Trauma & Stress)* (1st ed.). PESI.

Moore, C. (2016). *Namaslay: Rock Your Yoga Practice, Tap Into Your Greatness, & Defy Your Limits* (1). Victory Belt Publishing.

N. (2021). *Yoga as Medicine (07) by Journal, Yoga - McCall, Timothy [Paperback (2007)]*. Bantam, Paperback(2007).

PhD, M. B., Ampel, C., & PhD, F. T. (2018). *The Self Confidence Workbook: A Guide to Overcoming Self-Doubt and Improving Self-Esteem* (Workbook ed.). Althea Press.

Rachman, M. B. (2014). *Yoga's Touch Hands On Adjustments, Alignment and Verbal Cues*. Sacred Nectar Publishing.

Rountree, S., DeSiato, A., & Lee, C. (2019). *Teaching Yoga Beyond the Poses: A Practical Workbook for Integrating Themes, Ideas, and Inspiration into Your Class* (Workbook ed.). North Atlantic Books.

Shrivastava, & Martens. (2020). *A Practical Guide to Yoga Sequencing*. Www.Yogahumans.Com. https://www.yogahumans.com/downloads

Sincero. (2013). *You are a Badass*. Running Press.

Stauffer, K. A. (2010). *Anatomy & Physiology for Psychotherapists: Connecting Body & Soul* (Illustrated ed.). W. W. Norton & Company.

Stephens, Mark ((2010). *Teachign Yoga: Essential Foundations and Techniques*. North Atlantic Books.

Swanson, Anna (2019). *Science of Yoga: Understand the*

Anatomy and Physiology to Perfect Your Practice. DK Penguin Random House.

Theme Weaver: Connect the Power of Inspiration to Teaching Yoga by Michelle Berman Marchildon (2013) *Perfect Paperback.* (2021). Wildhorse Ventures LLC.

Wynne-Jones, G., Cowen, J., Jordan, J. L., Uthman, O., Main, C. J., Glozier, N., & van der Windt, D. (2013). Absence from work and return to work in people with back pain: a systematic review and meta-analysis. *Occupational and Environmental Medicine,* 71(6), 448–456. https://doi.org/10.1136/oemed-2013-101571

ACKNOWLEDGMENTS

This book could not have been possible without the support and assistance from my editor, friend, and fellow yogi, Mia Walshaw. You helped me dot my I's and cross my T's. You encouraged me to stick with it when I was ready to give up. You made my project "come to life" and I will be forever grateful to you for your encouraging texts, your meticulous attention to detail, and your friendly calls and invites for a game of chess or a trip to the nail salon to help me get my mind off of things.

I would also like to thank the many wonderful yoga teachers at my studio that continue to inspire me with their creative sequencing, words of wisdom, and opportunities to explore, expand, and release.

Finally, I'd like to thank my family for putting up with me throughout countless hours of preparing and planning my yoga sequences. You have heard me say "inhale mountain pose" so many times that it has become the inside joke at our house. Thank you to my husband for reminding me that I will always feel better after yoga. How true that is.

Thank you to everyone I have met on my yoga journey. Writing this book has helped me become a better teacher.

ABOUT THE AUTHOR

 Jen Vallens is an award winning, published writer. With a background in marketing and a passion for teaching and inspiring others, she has developed varied interests that serve her community.

She is a registered yoga teacher (RYT) with 500+ hours of yoga teacher training. She teaches yoga to a wide variety of students and uses her training to facilitate mental health support groups for those in treatment and recovery.

Jen is also the founder of OFF da ROOK Entertainment, an organization that runs scholastic chess tournaments throughout Southern California.

When not practicing yoga or running her chess business, she and her husband enjoy making wine and can be contacted through www.freedomwinecompany.com. Jen and her husband have two teenage sons and reside in Thousand Oaks, California.

You can also find Jen here:
https://www.jenvallens.com/

Made in the USA
Middletown, DE
13 February 2022